SERIES EDITOR: TONY HOLM

OSPREY COMBAT AIRCR

US NAVY AND MARINE CORPS A-4 SKYHAWK UNITS OF THE VIETNAM WAR

PETER MERSKY

OSPREY
PUBLISHING

Front cover
On 23 May 1972, VA-55's Lt Dennis J Sapp launched with his wingman, Lt Ken Bray, from USS *Hancock* (CVA-19) on an *Iron Hand* mission to cover an Alpha strike against targets northeast of Haiphong, in North Vietnam. Sapp's section had two missions – to destroy a SAM site adjacent to the target and to silence a lethal cluster of SAM sites ringing Haiphong near the target area.

Sapp flew A-4F BuNo 154996, which was armed with two AGM-45 Shrike anti-SAM missiles and four Rockeye bomblet canisters. The A-4Fs had recently been equipped with the Target Identification Acquisition System, which allowed the pilot to centre the radar from the SAM site or flak battery on the cockpit radar, then look through the gunsight for tracking purposes to decide where and when to drop weapons. *Iron Hand* A-4s orbited over a known site, or between sites, at 10,000 ft, fired their Shrikes and then rolled in to drop ordnance. This arrangement permitted a much more direct attack instead of having to fire a Shrike from a greater distance as was the case for A-6 and A-7 crews.

Sapp detached his section from the main strike group to go on ahead, and it was soon the target of two SAMs fired from the Haiphong area. He and his wingman immediately began evasive manoeuvres, narrowly evading the missiles. Sapp then continued on toward his assigned area. Although the site was well hidden, he pinpointed it and delivered two Rockeye canisters, all the while under defensive fire from 37 mm flak sites. Sapp destroyed all five radar vans in the centre of the site and his wingman despatched three SAMs on their launchers. Fires and explosions followed the two aviators as they left the area. Sapp took a photo from 20 miles away that showed smoke billowing above 20,000 ft. The target had turned out to be a SAM storage area hidden in a mountainside.

Sapp took his section to their designated station and continued the mission, using their Shrikes and remaining Rockeyes to suppress defences around Haiphong and allow the strikers to hit their targets.

Sapp received the Distinguished Flying Cross for this mission (*Cover artwork by Mark Postlethwaite*)

Dedication

For Eliot and the two Dennys. The first two have gone on before, while the second Denny remains a friend from Pensacola days. All three flew and fought in the A-4 in Vietnam and survived.

First published in Great Britain in 2007 by Osprey Publishing, Midland House, West Way, Botley, Oxford, OX2 0PH, 443 Park Avenue South, New York, NY, 10016, USA. E-mail; info@ospreypublishing.com

ISBN 13: 978 1 84603 181 6

Edited by Tony Holmes
Page design by Tony Truscott
Aircraft Profiles by Jim Laurier and Scale Drawings by Mark Styling
Cover Artwork by Mark Postlethwaite
Index by Alan Thatcher
Originated by PDQ Digital Media Solutions
Printed in China through Bookbuilders

07 08 09 10 11   10 9 8 7 6 5 4 3 2 1

For a catalogue of all books published by Osprey please contact:
NORTH AMERICA
Osprey Direct, C/o Random House Distribution Center, 400 Hahn Road, Westminster, MD, 2115. E-mail: info@ospreydirect.com

ALL OTHER REGIONS
Osprey Direct UK, PO Box 140 Wellingborough, Northants, NN8 2FA, UK
E-mail: info@ospreydirect.co.uk
(www.ospreypublishing.com)

ACKNOWLEDGEMENTS
Besides those A-4 aviators whose experiences appear in these pages, the following individuals helped with photographic and information research – Fred Ameel, Dan Crawford and John Cassara of the History Division of the Marine Corps University, Jim Casey of the Marine Corps Aviation Association, Dottie Crebo, Marie Estocin, Roy Grossnick and Mark Evans of the Naval Aviation Historian's Office, Hill Goodspeed of the National Museum of Naval Aviation, Doug Siegfried and Jan Jacobs of the Tailhook Association, Robert L Lawson, Bob Paul, Norman Polmar, Robert 'Boom' Powell, Rosario 'Zip' Rausa, Warren Thompson, Dr Istvan Toperczer and Wanda Weichman. Thank you also to the following members of the Skyhawk Association – Johnny Bittick, Vic Britt, Leon Bryant, Mike Green, Tom Lannom, Dave Weber and, especially, Mark Williams and Gary Verver.

OSPREY COMBAT AIRCRAFT • 69

US NAVY AND MARINE CORPS A-4 SKYHAWK UNITS OF THE VIETNAM WAR

CONTENTS

INTRODUCTION

Very few people who have been in naval aviation, as well as groups of enthusiasts, during the past 50 years have not been acquainted in some fashion with the Skyhawk. The product of one of America's most important designers, Ed Heinemann (1908-1991), the A-4 was without a doubt the backbone of the US Navy's carrier-borne strike force until the middle 1960s. It was also extensively used by the Marine Corps for close air support into the 1970s, especially during the first half of the ten-year struggle in South-east Asia.

However, the A-4 did not receive the press coverage that the perhaps more glamorous F-4 Phantom II did. While the latter battled North Vietnamese MiGs, the A-4 and its pilots, supported by myriad groundcrewmen, hurled themselves at heavily defended targets up and down the South-east Asian peninsula, often paying a heavy price in lives and aircraft. Flying into vast thickets of anti-aircraft bursts mixed with huge surface-to-air missiles (SAMs) took great courage and skill, and to do so repeatedly during a carrier's tour of duty on the line, lasting for a six-month (or more) deployment, bespoke a depth of dedication and character that can only be wondered at.

Although other books on the A-4 have appeared over the years, they usually describe the Skyhawk's overall career. I wanted to focus on the jet's most intense period of action. It is fitting that Osprey publishes this book as part of the highly successful *Combat Aircraft* series, which has set new standards for such historical reporting.

'Scooter', 'Tinker Toy', 'Hot Rod' – the A-4's nicknames indicated the affection and respect in which it was held by its pilots and maintainers. I dare say the A-4 would appear on any short list of great post-World War 2 combat aircraft. Fifty years after its initial introduction, the Skyhawk still flies with several air forces around the world – indeed, its formal career with the US Navy has only recently ended. With just a few flights in the back seats of TA-4Js, myself, I remain impressed with its agility and tractability, as well as its cramped cockpit. Ed Heinemann truly made the most compact carrier bomber, so small it did not require folding wings. Yet, his 'Hot Rod' saw many conflicts during its career, not the least of which was the bloody, frustrating war in the sticky, hot arena of Vietnam.

Peter Mersky
Alexandria, Virginia
January 2007

Editor's Note
This volume is endorsed by the Skyhawk Association, membership of which is open to any individual with a passion for the A-4. The association has a website which can be viewed at www.skyhawk.org, and it can be contacted via e-mail at newsletter-editor@a4skyhawk.org.

WAR HEATS UP

The US Navy was no stranger to the South China Sea in the mid summer of 1964, as carrier task forces had been cruising its waters for several years. Douglas' A-4 Skyhawk had also patrolled the area since early 1961, with VA-153 and VA-155, embarked with CVG-15 in USS *Coral Sea* (CVA-43), patrolling off the Vietnamese coast in their A4D-2s (later A-4B), ready to answer the call for help from the Laotian government after communist Pathet Lao forces had achieved several military victories.

In June 1963 VA-144 A-4C BuNo 149561 recovers aboard *Constellation* while on a *Westpac* deployment

The growing conflict in the region centred on the fighting in Laos. US President John F Kennedy conducted many colourful television news conferences pointing to large easel-mounted maps explaining his administration's policy and educating the American population as to just where Laos, neighbouring Cambodia and other South-east Asian countries were. Meanwhile, A-4 squadrons such as VA-56, VA-113 and VA-144 began escorting unarmed Vought RF-8A and Douglas RA-3B reconnaissance flights over the contested areas.

By now, the A-4C had made its way into the fleet, supplementing and then replacing the 'Bravo'. The 'Charlie' had first flown in 1959, and included upgraded avionics that gave the jet a limited all-weather capability. It was the 'Charlie' that bore the lion's share of the early fighting, sharing duties with the oncoming A-4E. But until the 'Echo' had been produced in sufficient numbers to replace the A-4C, the earlier model saw considerable combat through 1968.

The A-4E was a further modification of the basic design that included a more powerful engine offering reduced fuel consumption, thus increasing the Skyhawk's range by 27 percent. The 'Echo' also boasted two more underwing stations for ordnance, increasing the little bomber's effectiveness in the close air support role, which certainly pleased the Marine Corps.

GULF OF TONKIN CONFRONTATION

In August 1964, two engagements between American and North Vietnamese naval units became known as the Gulf of Tonkin Incidents. The first, on 2 August, was the more definitive – the second, on the 4th, has since proven not to have actually occurred – and involved communist PT boats firing on the destroyer USS *Maddox* (DD-731), which returned fire, hitting one of the PTs and killing its commanding officer. An umbrella of F-8 Crusaders from the carrier USS *Ticonderoga* (CVA-14) then appeared and strafed the communist vessels.

Deck crewmen hunch down as an A-4E equipped with Zuni rocket pods is launched from *Ticonderoga* in August 1964

After the second incident, President Lyndon B Johnson ordered a retaliatory strike codenamed *Pierce Arrow*. USS *Constellation* (CVA-64) and *Ticonderoga* launched aircraft to hit targets along the North Vietnamese coast. With 'Tico's' VF-51 and VF-53 providing escort, 'Connie's' F-4s, A-1s, and A-4s struck PT boat bases at Loc Chao, Hon Gai and Quang Khe, as well as oil storage facilities and anti-aircraft batteries at Vinh.

Cdr (later Adm) Wesley L McDonald, CO of VA-56 from *Ticonderoga*, led his A-4Es against the oil tanks. The action intensified as the attackers left the dump spewing huge columns of thick, black smoke that rose above the ruptured tanks. Post-strike assessment listed eight gunboats and PT boats destroyed, with an additional 21 damaged. The tally also listed the oil storage dump as 90 percent destroyed.

It was the first official combat action for the A-4, but it had not been without cost. Flak had shot down two American aircraft – an A-1H of VA-145 and an A-4C of VA-144, both from *Constellation's* Air Wing 14. The pilot of the A-1, Lt(jg) Richard C Sather, was killed. He was the first of many Naval Aviators to die in the long war to come.

The pilot of the A-4, Lt(jg) Everett Alvarez Jr, was 'lucky', if what was to come could be called having luck. He had already made one run on a nest of PT boats right behind his flight leader, and squadron executive officer, Cdr Bob Nottingham. The XO then set up for a second attack with his remaining rockets, but Alvarez, a junior pilot on his first deployment, decided to try his cannon and set up for a strafing run. His fire struck the bridge of one of the boats and he reported pieces flying off.

Alvarez rejoined his flight lead and the XO took the section out of the area, skimming low over the countryside at barely 100 ft. Everything seemed fine as they sped out of harm's way, but Alvarez's jet shuddered and there was a bright, yellow flash on his left side as they flew over a ridge just before the sea. Smoke filled his cockpit as every warning light flashed red. The stick froze in his hands and he keyed his mike to tell his lead he had been hit by enemy fire. The A-4 banked left and Alvarez again called, 'I'm on fire and out of control!'

The Skyhawk continued rolling and he found himself inverted as he reached for the face curtain of his ejection seat. As the A-4 rolled upright, he pulled. In a few seconds he was in the water and facing what would be more than eight years as a prisoner of war – Alvarez was the first American aviator to be captured by the North Vietnamese. At first there were signals from his survival transmitter, and a US Air Force HU-16 Albatross amphibian was despatched from Da Nang to try to retrieve the Navy pilot. However, returning pilots reported that Alvarez had gone down over rough terrain – they did not realise that he had actually landed in the water, and that enemy troops were close by. With a successful rescue

unlikely, the HU-16 was recalled. The loss of his A-4C (BuNo 149578) also represented the first combat loss for the Skyhawk. There would be more to come.

The two losses notwithstanding, Washington was pleased with the results of the *Pierce Arrow* raid. An important North Vietnamese base and storage facility had been left in smoking ruins, sending Hanoi a strong message that the US was in South-east Asia to stay and was not to be trifled with. The naiveté on Capitol Hill and, once again, the lack of understanding of an Asian enemy was to doom American servicemen to more than eight years of combat, injury and death. However, for the next six months, the situation stayed at a slow simmer, and the Navy returned to its participation in the *Barrel Roll* series of reconnaissance flights over Laos, which at the time seemed the more troublesome area in the region.

In February 1965, *Coral Sea* and *Hancock* Skyraiders and Skyhawks flew against targets around the Mu Gia Pass, on the border of North Vietnam and Laos, to block enemy infiltration and supply routes. At first, these actions seemed to work, but the communists quickly repaired the damaged jungle roads and bridges and soon men and material were moving back and forth again. The Washington planners concluded that the overall objective of stopping the North Vietnamese from heading south had not been achieved, even with 134 strikes and many other support missions. Stronger measures were needed.

When communist mortars struck Pleiku, in the Central Highlands of South Vietnam, killing eight Americans and wounding 109 others, President Johnson ordered Operation *Flaming Dart* to strike back. Accordingly, on 7 February, aircraft from *Coral Sea* and *Hancock* attacked troop barracks at Dong Hoi, 20 miles north of the demilitarised zone (DMZ) that effectively divided North and South Vietnam. At first, the bad weather that plagued the region at this time of the year prevented the carriers from launching their strikes as planned. By noon, however, conditions had improved, and 49 A-4s and A-1s (20 aircraft from *Coral Sea* and 29 from *Hancock*) launched. USS *Ranger* (CVA-61) contributed 34 aircraft, sending them 15 miles inland against barracks at Vit Thu Lu.

Because of the low clouds and rain, the strikers ran in at very low level – only 700 ft above the ground. Lt Edward A Dickson of VA-155 from

Fifteen months after being photographed recovering aboard 'Connie' (on page 7), and a month after the Gulf of Tonkin incidents, BuNo 149561 is seen here with BuNo 149582 from VA-146 on one of the carrier's four elevators

Coral Sea felt his A-4E (BuNo 150075) shudder from a flak hit, and he asked his wingman to check him over as they started their attack run. Suddenly, Dickson's aircraft burst into flames when it was hit by 37 mm flak, the jet trailing a 50-ft stream of fire as it flew over the Kien River. The CO of VA-153 (VA-155's sister squadron), Cdr Peter Mongilardi Jr, heard Dickson call that he was staying with the burning Skyhawk to continue his attack on the Dong Hoi barracks.

Soon afterward, the young aviator dropped his bombs and turned for the water, but his A-4 was now completely engulfed in flames, forcing him to eject. Unfortunately, his parachute apparently did not deploy and he was considered lost at sea, killed in action. Twenty years later, in 1985, the Vietnamese returned his ID card. Lt Dickson received a posthumous Navy Cross in recognition of his dedication in staying with his jet and completing the mission. It was the first award of the Navy's highest citation for aerial action in Vietnam, and the first for an A-4 pilot.

Cdr Mongilardi lost his life on 25 June (in BuNo 149574). Now CAG of *Coral Sea's* air wing, he was brought down by flak as he rolled in to attack a bridge. Mongilardi had led a very colourful, albeit brief, combat career. On 29 March, his badly damaged A-4 was leaking so much fuel that it was not certain he could make it back to the carrier. However, a skilful A-3 tanker crew hooked up with the struggling Skyhawk and its pilot and 'towed' them back to the ship, Mongilardi disconnecting on finals to fly aboard. When he became CAG, Mongilardi was replaced as the CO of VA-153 by Cdr Harry E Thomas, who would himself be killed on a mission to find a SAM site barely five months later, on 13 August. Flying at low level to scout the area, his A-4C (BuNo 148475) was seen to take flak and roll inverted before crashing.

Returning to 7 February and *Flaming Dart*, the squadrons from *Hancock's* CVW-21 now rolled in on Dong Hoi. Seventeen A-4s from VA-212 and VA-216 dropped their ordnance and headed for the safety of the South China Sea. Battle damage assessment (BDA) photos by RF-8As showed that 16 buildings of the barracks complex had been destroyed and six damaged. The official assessment was that *Flaming Dart* had been 'at best a qualified and inadequate reprisal'.

The US strike did not have the desired affect. Even though President Johnson proclaimed he did not want to widen the war, the communists attacked a hotel in Qui Nhon that was being used as an enlisted men's quarters on 10 February, killing 23 American soldiers and wounding many more. Adm U S Grant Sharp, Commander in Chief, Pacific, called for a swift response, and *Flaming Dart II* began the next day.

On 11 February, the same three carriers (*Hancock* had been heading for the Philippines for refurbishment but was recalled) were tasked with strikes against the barracks at Chanh Hoa, with Dong Hoi as a secondary target if required. Unfortunately, like the previous strike, weather interfered. Planning for such a problem, the A-4s were loaded with Snakeye bombs, a so-called retarded bomb that would permit the aircraft that delivered the ordnance at low level to escape before it exploded.

With visibility barely a mile in low clouds, the strikers came in at 500 ft and ran into stiff enemy defensive fire. F-8s, F-4s and A-1s hit the enemy flak positions with Zuni rockets and 20 mm cannon fire, and the aircraft from *Ranger* led the attack. An F-8D of VF-154 from *Coral Sea* was brought down and its pilot, Lt Cdr Robert H Shumaker, was captured. VA-153's Lt William T Majors in A-4C BuNo 149572 was also lost. After climbing back to altitude following his attack run, his engine seized – it was never determined why – and he had to eject. A USAF helicopter picked up the Navy pilot and he was soon back with his squadron.

Another Skyhawk of VA-155 diverted to Da Nang with heavy battle damage, where Lt E G Hiebert made a wheels-up landing. He had come in with hung ordnance, some of which fell off and began to burn as he scrambled free of his aircraft. The fire closed the USAF base's main runway for several hours.

The tit-for-tat responses following the Gulf of Tonkin Incidents of early August 1964 yielded less than satisfactory results. The communists remained active, showing no signs of wanting to enter discussions to end the confrontation. For its part, the US had to be content with what it believed was a strong show of force to let the Hanoi government know it would not be easily pushed out of South-east Asia. In the meantime, both men and equipment began pouring into South Vietnam. Offshore, carrier task forces also started to put in long deployments.

VA-216 was not as well known as some other A-4 squadrons serving in Vietnam, but the 'Black Diamonds' saw their fair share of action from several carriers. Here, A-4C BuNo 147765 launches from *Hancock* in May 1965. This aircraft was subsequently transferred to the Argentine air force (as A-4Q C-312) in 1976-77 and saw action in the Falklands War of 1982, when it was damaged by British anti-aircraft fire. Having survived the conflict, the veteran jet was written off in a flying accident on 1 October 1991

At this time, the A-4 flew with every air wing, no matter the size of the aircraft carrier. The two main models were the A-4C and A-4E, with the 'Charlie' carrying a surprisingly large portion of the burden until replaced in greater numbers by the 'Echo' by 1968. The A-4C featured a lengthened nose from the earlier A-4B, as well as a slightly more powerful engine. The A-4E also had increased power, greater range and two more underwing ordnance stations, increasing its value as a weapon for close air support. The E-model would fly throughout the war and eventually perform some of the last combat missions with the Marine Corps squadron that remained in-theatre after the ceasefire in 1973.

As many as three 'Scooter' squadrons might be assigned to an air wing, while two remained when the A-6 Intruder arrived. Often, A-4s were paired with the slower, but powerful prop-driven A-1 Skyraiders – tried and tested attack aircraft that had earned their spurs in Korea 12 years earlier. However, being too slow to keep up with the modern jet air wing, the A-1 was on its way out – they had to be launched first to meet their rendezvous with the rest of the wing. By late 1967 only one squadron of single-seat Skyraiders remained in combat. But the aircraft certainly kept its colourful and well-earned reputation, as did its pilots and crews, even managing to down two North Vietnamese MiG-17s in 1965 and 1966.

The little A-4 was having an incredible baptism of fire. The missions, and daily anticipation of them, harkened back to the gritty days of World War 2 and Korea as squadrons lost aircraft and pilots at alarming rates.

Crewmen aboard *Hancock* prepare an A-4E of VA-212 for launch in March 1965. Note the horizontal plate just below the rescue arrow and above the wing-mounted cannon. It prevented gases released when the cannon was fired from being ingested into the aircraft's air intake and stalling the engine

STEEP LEARNING CURVE

After the *Flaming Dart* strikes in February 1965, the US military began building up a tremendous presence in South-east Asia. Similar to June 1950, when UN forces were caught unprepared by North Korea's invasion of South Korea, the US was also caught off guard in Vietnam, but was aided by a loose alliance that involved the countries of the region such as South Korea, Thailand and Australia. The United States rapidly funnelled huge amounts of arms and people into the tiny, struggling country of South Vietnam.

What had started as a system of advisors and training facilities for the South Vietnamese military soon became a huge conglomeration owned and operated by Americans, both military and civilian. It was not the best way to run a war, particularly when it quickly became clear that the government in Washington was not about to let its field commanders do their jobs.

President Johnson took his fairly significant victory in the 1964 election as a mandate to do what he wanted, and he opened the floodgates to send thousands of servicemen and their weapons to South-east Asia. He and his ethereal Secretary of Defense, Robert S McNamara, also believed that the war would be better prosecuted from the Pentagon rather than from the flightdecks in the South China Sea or the paddies and jungles in-country. It was a tragic series of wrong decisions that doomed the war from the beginning, much to the horrified consternation of those who fought it.

A-4E BuNo 150130 of VA-212 taxis past F-8Cs of VF-24 aboard USS *Hancock*. This Skyhawk was lost to flak on 26 March 1965 when CVW-21 attacked the radar site at Vinh Son. Its pilot, Cdr K L Shugart, ejected and was rescued by a USAF SAR helicopter (*via Tom Irwin*)

An A-3B from VAH-8 services bomb-laden A-4s of VA-23 heading toward North Vietnam. Both squadrons were from *Midway*, which saw limited action during the war

THUNDER BEGINS TO ROLL

With the disappointing results of the *Flaming Dart* missions, Washington planners created *Rolling Thunder* – a long campaign of

attacks that began with targets near the demilitarised zone (DMZ) dividing the two Vietnams and 'rolled' north to Hanoi. The hope was that after such a prolonged series of strikes that eventually threatened North Vietnam's capital, the communists would come to the bargaining table. It might have been a good plan on paper, but once again high-level meddling threw things into disarray and ultimately kept the US in a no-win situation for four years.

And all the while, the carrier air wings flew into some of the worst concentrations of ground fire ever seen in the 50+ years of aerial warfare.

To the frustration of most senior military commanders, both Navy and Air Force, severe restrictions were imposed. For example, no strike could be flown without prior administration approval.

Two geographic points in the South China Sea were established for the carrier task forces. *Yankee Station* served as a central location for operations against North Vietnam. *Dixie Station* to the south was created shortly thereafter at the request of Army Gen William Westmoreland. He was so impressed by the Navy's carrier support of infantry operations that he asked for a permanent carrier presence off South Vietnam. This position was all the more necessary because of a lack of proper land bases from which ground support aircraft could operate.

The Army general's request, while complementary, added to the Navy's burden, requiring ships to stay at sea much longer than the normal line period to service both stations. In June 1965, the Navy had to deploy no less than five carriers to accomplish its tasks. *Dixie Station* evolved into a 'warm up' area for newly arrived carrier air wings. In the relatively 'peaceful' atmosphere of the southern war zone, where communist air defence was at a minimum, 'green' aircrews could get their feet wet, get used to dropping bombs and strafing and experience the unrelenting pressure of daily combat operations, before going north into the 'real' world of AAA, missiles, MiGs and the threat of shootdown and capture.

Rolling Thunder was supposed to start on 20 February, barely ten days after the second *Flaming Dart* raid. However, a failed coup in South Vietnam and subsequent bad weather kept postponing the initial operation. It was not until 2 March that the first *Rolling Thunder* strikes were launched, sending USAF and (South) Vietnamese Air Force (VNAF) aircraft into southern North Vietnam. The Navy's role was that of intelligence-gathering reconnaissance, codenamed *Blue Tree*.

The Navy's first *Rolling Thunder* missions came on 15 March, with aircraft from *Hancock* and *Ranger* hitting the ammunition depot at Phu Qui, half way between Vinh and Thanh Hoa. Sixty-four A-4s and A-1s struck in the early afternoon, preceded by eight F-8Cs, which softened up enemy air defences, and two RF-8As, which took appropriate BDA photos. The strike aircraft still had to negotiate heavy defensive fire – 37 mm, automatic weapons and small arms – to drop their Mk 81 250-lb bombs, fire their Zuni rockets and strafe with their 20 mm cannons. A VA-95 A-1H from *Ranger* ditched after leaving the target area and its young pilot, Lt(jg) Charles F Clydesdale, was lost. The results of this first Navy *Rolling Thunder* raid were considered a limited success. In coming days, additional attacks included aircraft from *Coral Sea* and *Hancock*.

The *Barrel Roll* programme was also refined because of less than satisfactory achievements. This lack of production was ascribed to the

A-4C BuNo 149574 from the 'Blue Tail Flies' of VA-153 launches from USS *Coral Sea* on 24 March 1965. The aircraft carries Mk 84 2000-lb bombs as well as the normal 300-gallon fuel tank. This aircraft was brought down by AAA northwest of Thanh Hoa three months later on 25 June while being flown by CVW-15 CAG, and ex-VA-153 CO, Cdr Peter Mongilardi. The latter failed to eject from the jet and was killed, thus becoming the first CAG to be lost in action in the Vietnam War (*PH1 James F Falk*)

Soviet-supplied SA-2 SAMs quickly became one of the two greatest threats to American strike groups throughout the Vietnam War. Relatively mobile and lethal, the big 35-ft missiles could be launched from nearly any level area that could accommodate the launcher and its various support vans that helped aim and fire each SAM (*Gabor Palfai via Istvan Toperczer*)

tight control coming from Washington, which required lots of approval time against the transitory targets that infiltrated the various supply trails that were the main interest of the operation. The choke points were therefore given added attention. A-4s and A-1s bombarded these vulnerable areas – especially the Mu Gia Pass – from late February through March, with the Navy participating in 23 of the 43 new *Barrel Roll* missions, flying 275 sorties.

By April, more attention was being given to the fighting in South Vietnam, where increasingly bold Viet Cong (VC) guerrillas were giving the Army of the Republic of Vietnam a hard time. Aircraft from *Midway, Coral Sea* and the anti-submarine (ASW) carrier USS *Yorktown* (CVS-10), positioned at *Dixie Station* east of Cam Ranh Bay, hit VC positions northwest of Saigon.

Part of the vast infusion of men and supplies was the arrival of the first formal units of the Marine Corps, hailed with much fanfare, with a fully blown amphibious landing on the beaches of Da Nang. The troops stormed ashore, rifles at the ready, only to be met by smiling local girls who draped flowered leis around the necks of the bemused 'Leathernecks' – Iwo Jima had never been like this! Accompanying the 'assault' by the grunts was the arrival of several Marine Corps aircraft squadrons.

April also saw the first discovery of enemy SAM sites. The Soviet Union had supplied North Vietnam with SA-2s – the same weapon that had knocked CIA pilot Gary F Powers' high-flying U-2 spyplane out of the sky in May 1960. The missile had also accounted for another U-2 over Cuba during the missile crisis of October 1962. Besides propaganda, haughty instructors and training in the USSR, nations deemed friendly by the Soviets also received a huge amount of weaponry in the form of jet fighters and now, by the mid-1960s, the dangerous SA-2.

On 5 April 1965, an RF-8A from the VFP-63 det aboard *Coral Sea* brought back photos of the first SAM site to be properly identified. The site was only 15 miles southeast of Hanoi, and its discovery sent shivers down the spines of task force commanders and line aviators alike. A second site was found in May, and by July several sites had been discovered. However, it wasn't until the Navy and Air Force lost a few jets to the SA-2s that official permission was given to attack the sites, thereby starting the anti-SAM mission that soon became known as *Iron Hand*.

The first aircraft lost to a SAM was a USAF F-4C on 24 July. One

Bedecked with 36 mission markings, VA-72's A-4E BuNo 149993 is ready to launch from *Independence*. This aircraft was later lost in a non-fatal operational accident on 27 May 1970 over the South China Sea while serving with VA-152 aboard USS *Shangri-La* (CVS-38)

Oriskany ploughs through the South China Sea, its flightdeck crowded with aircraft. A-1s take up the aft portion, while A-4s share space with F-8s. A Skyhawk rests on the bow elevator aft of the '34' hull number

pilot was killed and the other captured. The first Navy loss to the missile was VA-23 A-4C BuNo 148564 on 13 August. Its pilot, Lt W E Newman, ejected and was rescued by a destroyer.

Hunting for SAM sites began immediately, but it was not until 17 October that an actual strike mission (codenamed *Iron Hand*) was flown. Four VA-72 A-4Es from USS *Independence* (CVA-62), with the pathfinding services of an A-6A Intruder from VA-75, found a site near the MiG airfield at Kep. Cdr H B Southworth, VA-72 CO, duly led his Skyhawks against the communist missile battery.

With SAMs rapidly deploying in increasing numbers, US aircraft were forced to fly at lower altitudes, which put them within reach of flak batteries and even small arms fire. Soon, some of the older veterans who had flown during World War 2 were saying that the flak over Hanoi and Haiphong was worse than the barrages they had seen over Berlin or Tokyo in 1945.

Throughout 1965, the carrier air wings learned the rules and art of modern war. After all, it had been more than a decade since American aircrews had fought a sustained campaign. The learning curve was steep, and costly. Along with other types, the A-4 squadrons lost aircraft and men, some killed, others captured and imprisoned.

Perhaps one of the most famous PoWs was Cdr James B Stockdale, a Crusader fighter pilot who had been the first aviator to achieve the significant milestone of 1000 hours in Vought's world-beater. He had also served a tour as a test pilot. Stockdale had been on station during the Gulf of Tonkin Incident as CO of VF-51, and had led his squadron in the early retaliatory operations against the North Vietnamese.

In April 1965, Stockdale again deployed, this time as the air wing commander of CVW-16 aboard the *Essex*-class carrier USS *Oriskany* (CVA-34). The 'O-boat', as she was sometimes called, was one of six modernised carriers designated as 27C, or '27 Charlies', in the lexicon of naval aviation. Built at the close of World War 2 and decommissioned, the vessel was recommissioned and made a single combat cruise during the Korean War, operating F2H Banshees and F9F Panthers. Now, *Oriskany* departed the US for the first of eight combat deployments in South-east Asia.

As wing commander – the exact title was Commander, Carrier Air Wing, but the more evocative designation of 'CAG' from World War 2 days remained (and still does) the commonly accepted name – Stockdale had responsibility for nine squadrons and squadron detachments. Although he naturally flew a lot of missions in F-8s, he also flew A-4s. Sampling different types within his wing was a CAG's prerogative and pleasure that came with the senior rank.

On 9 September, Stockdale manned an A-4E from VA-163 to lead a strike against the troublesome, almost legendary, Thanh Hoa railway bridge. But weather made the original plan unworkable and Stockdale sent the various elements out looking for secondary targets.

'I had neglected to mention to Wynn Foster (XO of VA-163) what exactly our alternate target would be', Stockdale later recalled for *Carrier Air Group Commanders* by Robert L Lawson. 'We loitered offshore listening to VA-163 CO Henry Jenkins' division comparing notes on their detection of SAM radars on their just-acquired gear, flying in the soup down near Vinh. I knew of a place where we could normally get rid of a bomb load into a worthwhile target without prior arrangements, and with surprisingly little flak. It was a railroad siding four or five miles west of Highway 1'.

Stockdale was about 15 miles south of the bridge. Cdr Foster followed a mile behind, watching the CAG set up for his attack on the railroad siding.

'I didn't even have my oxygen mask snapped across my face. We were coming in flat, in trail, right on the deck at about 500+ indicated. I, and undoubtedly Wynn, both totally relaxed. I had pulled this foul-weather snakeye manoeuvre on this same train parking area a couple of days before and got no flak.'

But flak had begun to blossom as Stockdale came in very low – perhaps as low as 150 ft – and released his bombs. As he climbed through 700 ft, he felt his A-4E (BuNo 151134) get hit from ground fire. It was quickly evident that he had no control as the doomed Skyhawk pitched up then dived for the ground. Having frantically tried to reconnect his oxygen mask so that he could call Cdr Foster, Stockdale then ejected. He thus became only the second CAG to be lost during the war.

Foster called for SAR support. Stockdale's A-4 had crashed on a tidal flat as its pilot floated beneath his parachute toward a North Vietnamese village. At one point, Foster

Photographs of Cdr James Stockdale in flight gear are rare. Here, he descends from an A-4 during the 1965 cruise that eventually saw him eject into captivity

The second most feared part of the North Vietnamese arsenal was the wide assortment of anti-aircraft guns. This ZPU-2 twin-mount 14.5 mm machine gun is manned by two militiawomen (*via Istvan Toperczer*)

prepared to strafe the village to protect Stockdale. He armed his cannon and roared over the huts at 400
knots, but there was little he could
do. Stockdale was quickly captured
and began one of the most incredible stories of wartime survival ever
experienced by an American fighting man. He spent seven-and-a-half
years in Hanoi and eventually
received the Medal of Honor, retiring as a vice admiral. Foster returned
to *Oriskany* after radioing that SAR
could not help the CAG now.

The 100 mm flak gun was among
the heaviest anti-aircraft weapons
in the North Vietnamese arsenal.
This photograph was taken during
an actual engagement near
Haiphong in 1965 (*via Istvan
Toperczer*)

When Cdr Pete Mongilardi was lost on 25 June, he was replaced as
CAG 15 by Cdr Wesley L McDonald, who had led VA-56 during the
Gulf of Tonkin Incidents. After refresher carrier training in the A-4,
McDonald made his way to the combat zone courtesy of *Hancock*, which
was heading in the same direction. Nearing the Philippines, the new
CAG 15 took advantage of an A-3 to fly aboard *Coral Sea* and assume
his new command. The next day, McDonald became 'embroiled in
the terribly frustrating business of fighting a politically constrained
war, which was being directed most heavily by the political/military
leadership half a world away with little, if any, input from the on-scene
commanders'.

By late 1965, several A-4s had been shot down, their pilots killed or
captured. Another *Oriskany* loss was that of Lt Cdr Trent R Powers, the
operations officer of VA-164. Powers had taken his A-4E (BuNo
151173), complete with his own Mk 82 500-lb bombs, to the Royal Thai
Air Base at Takhli on 30 October. The USAF, frustrated at its inability to
deal with the growing number of SAMs, had lost several F-105
Thunderchiefs and F-4 Phantom IIs to the big missiles – four from one
squadron alone in the first half of October.

The Air Force had no radar homing capabilities or warning gear. Navy
A-4s, however, carried the APR-23, a device that detected SAM fire-
control radar signals, pinpointing the missile site's location. Strike plans
called for two flights of four 'Thuds' each, led by Lt Cdr Powers. Each
F-105 would carry eight 750-lb bombs. During the brief, Powers wanted
to fly at 50 ft and skip-bomb the target. The 'Thud' crews wanted to dive-
bomb the SAM sites, saying that going down vertically would offer less of
a target for the gunners on the ground. Powers was amenable – he would
make the first pass anyway, and would be well out of the area before the
Air Force went in.

The strike force launched the next day, 31 October. At first it seemed
like weather was going to make finding the target difficult, if not
impossible. However, Lt Cdr Powers ordered the F-105s to assume an
attack 'V' and he led them through the overcast. The group finally broke
out under the clouds, flying in a scattered formation. Each pilot hung on
to the man in front of him as they threaded their way through the tunnel
of hills on either side. It was not for the faint-hearted, this mission that
covered more than 600 miles.

By now there was ground fire, which struck some of the 'Thuds', but everyone pressed on, waiting for Powers' little magic box to tell them where the SAMs were. Besides the flak, there were missiles in the air, 15 at one count.

'I've got 'em on my nose', Powers finally called as he began his attack run. He flew right over the target and dropped his bombs. Unfortunately, his Skyhawk was badly damaged and seemed to be coming apart. Powers was seen to eject, and there were reports that he had been spotted on the ground. There were even signals reportedly coming from his SAR beeper. However, the weather made rescue that far into North Vietnam impossible. Powers was posted missing in action (MIA). As has so often been the case concerning Vietnam MIAs, final determination of Trent Powers' MIA status was resolved when the Vietnamese returned remains that were identified as his.

After the F-105 pilots made it back to Takhli, they demanded the Air Force give their Navy compatriot the Air Force Cross, the service's highest award. The colonel who commanded the base balked. The incensed 'Thud' crews tried to enlist the help of a visiting general, who told the colonel to follow through. Although nothing came of it, the Navy did award Powers the Navy Cross for his exceptional leadership and dedication at the cost of his life. He was also posthumously promoted to captain.

As has been noted, the carrier *Independence* arrived in the South China Sea in June 1965, bringing with it CVW-7, which included A-4E squadrons VA-72 and VA-86. Although carriers were normally assigned

Lt Cdr Trent Powers (left) indulges in traditional pilot-to-pilot conversation with Lt Steward in VA-164's ready room aboard *Oriskany*. Powers received a posthumous Navy Cross following his exploits leading USAF F-105s against communist SAM sites on 31 October 1965

Independence's flightdeck is a busy place as crewmen ready an A-4E from VA-86 for a strike into North Vietnam on 7 July 1965

Three A-4Cs from VA-94 are directed forward towards the bow of *Enterprise* on 3 December 1965 following the completion of the first combat mission flown from a nuclear carrier. To the left, bombed up A-4Cs from VA-93 await the next launch cycle

Right
With a buddy refuelling pack on his jet's centreline station, VA-22's Lt(jg) Tom Murray taxis A-4C BuNo 149490 towards the catapult for a tanker mission from *Midway* in May 1965. This aircraft was lost in action three months later on 24 August when its pilot, Lt(jg) Richard Brunhaver, experienced control restrictions when he attempted to pull out after diving on a road bridge near Phong Bai. The jet glanced off a karst ridge and then began to climb away, having suffered serious structural damage. A veteran of more than 100 missions, Brunhaver soon realised that his A-4 was unflyable and he ejected into captivity (*PH2 Karl Medberg*)

to either the Atlantic or Pacific fleets for several years, the long war in South-east Asia required that ships from the Atlantic side occasionally visit the war zone to augment or relieve Pacific fleet units. The assignment of 'Indy' for its only combat cruise added a fifth carrier and its air wing to the fighting.

Another carrier entered the war zone on 2 December. She was big and she was a 'nuke'. USS *Enterprise* (CVAN-65) brought with it CVW-9, which was an especially large air wing with no less than four A-4C squadrons – VAs 36, 76, 93 and 94 – besides her two F-4 squadrons, an A-6 squadron, and assorted detachments. She was the largest warship built up to that time, and she brought a combination of new technology and imposing physical presence to the Tonkin Gulf.

Some people felt that bringing so many aircraft – this cruise would be the only time that four A-4 squadrons would be embarked aboard one ship – was an effort to put more than 100 aircraft on the new carrier to demonstrate its ability to bring a large number of weapons and personnel to the war zone.

Following an initial work-up on *Dixie Station, Enterprise* launched strikes against North Vietnam on 17 December, setting the record for a day's total with 165 combat sorties, surpassing *Kitty Hawk's* 131.

On 22 December, a 100-aeroplane Alpha strike hit the Uong Bi thermal power plant 15 miles north of Haiphong. The term 'Alpha' referred to the 'A-list' of targets that usually required a major effort of a large number of aircraft. Three carriers sent their air wings out – *Enterprise, Kitty Hawk* and *Ticonderoga*, now on its second war cruise. This was the first time that an industrial target would be hit instead of the bases and support installations that had been the usual recipients of Navy attention.

The *Enterprise* strike force went feet dry and swung around from the north while the other two carriers' bombers approached from the south. When the attackers left the scene, they reported the power plant sending up pillars of oily, black smoke. The raid was considered a success – the plant was down for several months.

Two A-4s from CVW-9 were lost on the Uong Bi strike, one from VA-76 and another from VA-36. Lt John D Prudhomme was killed when his aircraft hit the ground as his section made its run-in to the target. It was thought he had been hit by flak and perhaps wounded. Soon afterwards, the VA-36 A-4s began their run. Lt(jg) Wendell R Alcorn was wounded as he set himself up for his attack, his oxygen mask catching fire.

Lt F C Spellman of VA-22 launches 2.75-inch rockets from his A-4C (BuNo 147759) during a practice mission off *Dixie Station*. This aircraft was one of two Skyhawks from VA-76 downed by AAA on 14 July 1967. Both pilots survived

He had to get out, and he ejected and was quickly captured. Alcorn spent the next seven years as a PoW.

Another *Enterprise* A-4 was lost the following day when VA-94's Lt(jg) William L Shankel went down during an attack on the Hai Duong Bridge. Shankel's aircraft was hit just as he dropped his bombs and pulled up. As smoke and flames filled his little jet's cockpit, he too ejected into captivity.

In November, in an effort to smooth out some scheduling rough spots, North Vietnam was sectioned into six 'route packages'. Although not hard and fast, the Navy had particular responsibility for Route Pack VIB, which included the country's principal harbour of Haiphong, nearly due east of Hanoi.

As he would throughout the war, President Johnson now instituted a 'bombing halt' beginning on 24 December to entice the North Vietnamese to talk peace. It was a forlorn hope, for the communists had absolutely no intention of talking peace. They had dug in for the long haul, and it would be some considerable time before the US realised that hard fact. The bombing halt lasted for a month.

During this first phase of *Rolling Thunder*, the Seventh Fleet's carrier aircraft had flown some 31,000 sorties, dropped 64,000 bombs of various types and fired 128,500 rockets.

This first full year of the Vietnam War had also seen the Navy lose 22 A-4s as a result of combat, with many others written off in so-called operational accidents – mechanical malfunction and pilot error. The downing of VA-144's Lt(jg) Alvarez in 1964 brought total combat losses to 23.

Carrier Skyhawk Marines, 1965. The pilots of H&MS-15 Det N pose beside A-4C BuNo 147681, nicknamed *"Fanny Hill"* – all four of the Det's jets were named after women with dubious morals! Making a deployment to Vietnam aboard USS *Hornet* (CVS-12), these Marine aviators provided aerial protection for the ASW carrier. The bird silhouette and the designation 'VMA 22' on the fuselage is a nod to VA-22, which had previously hosted the squadron aboard *Midway*

'YV 83' *"Mamie Stover"* (BuNo 147829) carries more than 30 mission markings, indicating that this Marine 'Scooter' had seen action over South Vietnam besides its regularly assigned CAP duties. Note the mission markings on the intake and the early AIM-9 Sidewinder missile on station 3 under the right wing. The jet is being led up the deck of *Hornet* by a tillerman, who has his steering bar attached to the A-4 by its nose wheel. This aircraft was lost in a mid-air collision with A-4C BuNo 147828 on 8 November 1968 while serving with east coast Replacement Air Group unit VA-44, based at NAS Jacksonville

THE WAR ESCALATES

T he carrot of a bombing halt was not working. The North Vietnamese were not coming to the peace talks. For 37 days Task Force 77 operations were drastically reduced, but all the enemy did was use the time to reconstruct bridges and bases and bring in new supplies of shells, SAMs and MiGs, which they had received from the USSR. Flak batteries were added along the corridor between Hanoi and Haiphong and the border with China. The skies of North Vietnam were quickly becoming the most dangerous in the history of aerial warfare.

As the US government planned for the resumption of the bombing campaign, the dismal monsoon that so affected the area at this time of the year was at its height. Rain, clouds and wind blanketed the South-east Asia coast, reaching far out into the South China Sea where the carriers orbited *Yankee* and *Dixie Stations*.

On 14 January 1966, Lt(jg) S B Jordon of VA-36 had to eject as he approached *Enterprise* for landing. His A-4C (BuNo 147753) had been hit by AAA over Laos and was streaming valuable fuel. Both wings and his landing gear doors had been damaged. However, with one bomb still hung on a rack, it was not worth the risk of bringing the shot up Skyhawk back aboard. Jordan punched out and was quickly rescued.

The bombing campaign against the North resumed on 31 January when *Kitty Hawk* and *Ranger* sent in their aircraft. Bridges and waterways were the main targets. *Ranger's* VA-55 struck a ferry crossing, running in under low clouds. Lt Cdr S G Chumley made a pass over some barges and dropped his bombs. As he pulled up, flak found his A-4E (BuNo 152066), and as his aircraft went out of control, he ejected. He was rescued by a Navy helicopter.

Cdr Hubert B Loheed, the CO of VA-146, and also from *Ranger's* CVW-14, was not so fortunate. Leading his four A-4Cs against river barges south of Vinh, Loheed went into the low clouds but did not come out. In fact, he was not seen again until the North Vietnamese returned his remains in 1994. He had been probably been hit by flak and perhaps, wounded and in-capacitated, he crashed during his weapons delivery dive.

Ranger makes a turn on *Yankee Station*. The size of the vessel's flightdeck is definitely shown to advantage as compared to the smaller 27C carriers. Note the plane guard destroyer trailing in the vessel's wake. Although all four ships of the *Forrestal* class deployed to Vietnam, the Atlantic Fleet's *Saratoga*, *Independence* and namesake CVA-59 made only one combat cruise each. The Pacific Fleet's *Ranger* made six (*via Robert Dunn*)

Conducting the war was nothing if not a fluid exercise. There were suspected bomb shortages, as well as shortages of personal survival radios, which could make the difference between rescue and capture for a pilot on the ground. The air wings also routinely endured the adjustment of route package responsibilities. One such change saw *Yankee Station* moved farther north to bring the carrier strike groups closer to their targets. Of course, the station was only a geographic point, plotted on charts – carrier groups moved constantly throughout the South China Sea, using *Yankee Station* merely as a reference and anchor.

As the monsoon abated in late March, the pace of the *Rolling Thunder* schedule increased. Instead of hitting waterways, mining rivers and taking out the odd supply train, the air wings were given an increased list of potential targets that focused on the roads and railways linking the harbour of Haiphong with the central point of the capital Hanoi.

On 13 April aircraft from *Ticonderoga's* CVW-5 attacked the Haiphong railway bridge. 'Tico' had lost four A-4s since the resumption of *Rolling Thunder*, including one flown by the CAG, Cdr Jack L Snyder, who had ejected and been rescued. He was flying an A-4C (BuNo 149557) from VA-144 on one of the innumerable road reconnaissance hops when his aircraft was hit by a SAM. Fighting for control of his burning jet, Cdr Snyder flew more than 60 miles before punching out.

At this point, the restrictions against strategic industrial targets such as electric and petroleum facilities were gradually lifted, and the war soon escalated into a huge offensive series of strikes. The A-4 squadrons found themselves right in the middle of it, and aeroplanes and pilots were soon 'going Downtown' into the heart of the crisscrossing network of SAMs and flak batteries defending Hanoi and Haiphong. 'Downtown' referred to a popular song of the time, sung by British star Petula Clark. It was an ironic take on the lyrics that promised 'Everything's waiting for you downtown', and for the men of the carrier strike groups, it was.

THE POL CAMPAIGN BEGINS

Perhaps the most important development in 1966 was the start of the so-called POL (petroleum, oil, lubricants) campaign in June. On-scene commanders seemed to be the only people who understood that the North Vietnamese ability to make war could be badly hurt if strikes were made on their POL industry and storage facilities. It was a basic fact of war – hit the enemy's oil lifeline and you hit him where it hurt. However, the politicians in Washington were having difficulty understanding the meaning of the reconnaissance photographs brought back by the RA-5Cs and RF-8As. In 1965 and into the early portion of 1966, the North Vietnamese had been busily establishing large POL storage farms around Hanoi and, especially, Haiphong.

Finally, in April, *someone* made a decision to begin *Rolling Thunder 50* – a series of attacks against North Vietnam's POL and railway systems. The bridges that linked Haiphong to Hanoi and other portions of the country were vital conduits that had to be destroyed if the flow of supplies south was to be interrupted, or stopped.

However, uncertainty as well as undue caution in Washington about what targets would be hit, and the risk of strike aircraft damaging peripheral areas that might involve other countries' people and assets,

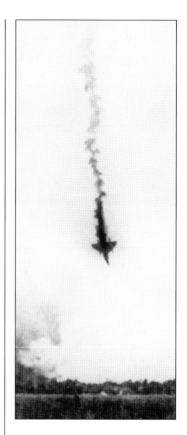

Cdr John Abbott's A-4C BuNo 148512 was hit in the right wing by flak while the CO of VA-113 was leading eight aircraft against the Vinh Son road bridge on 20 April 1966. Although he succeeded in coaxing the burning jet towards the coast, it eventually started to roll uncontrollably and disintegrate, at which point Abbott ejected. The aircraft is seen here diving toward the ground soon after being abandoned by its pilot. Having been made CO of VA-113 just nine days earlier, Cdr Abbott died soon after being captured – presumably of wounds sustained when his jet was hit by flak, or injuries suffered when he ejected. A SAR operation was mounted shortly after Abbott's jet went down, and during the course of this operation VA-113's A-4C BuNo 149495, flown by Lt(jg) H G Welch, was also hit by AAA. The pilot managed to get all the way back to *Kitty Hawk* before an internal fire burned through his flight controls and he was forced to eject. Welch was quickly rescued by the ship's plane guard UH-2 Seasprite (*via Istvan Toperczer*)

postponed the original kick-off until June – some two months later!

Finally, on 29 June, *Ranger* sent its aircraft to bomb Haiphong's POL complex. Flying an F-4B, Cdr (later RAdm) Frederick F Palmer led the CVW-14 strike. A-4Cs from VA-55 and VA-146 dived toward the massive layout of tanks and bunkers. When they left, the facility was engulfed in smoke and flames. The initially heavy flak had been largely silenced by the F-4s of VF-142, while its sister squadron, VF-143 provided TARCAP services, watching for MiGs.

Technically, strike lead was VA-146 CO Cdr Al Schaufelberger

– a highly capable and respected aviator. Some of his pilots thought he was short-changed when Cdr Palmer received the Navy Cross while others got a DFC. As always, politics played a role in the awards system.

Constellation's CVW-9 also contributed its share of destruction on the 29th, hitting the Do Son POL farm just south of the main harbour. The next day, *Hancock's* aircraft teamed with those of *Constellation* for a strike against the facility at Bac Giang. Other attacks followed on 1 July. The entire coastal assembly of North Vietnam's strategic oil industry and reserves seemed to be going up in flames.

Despite heavy flak and SAMs, only one A-4 was lost during the course of these three strikes. On 1 July, the CO of 'Connie's' VA-155, Cdr Charles H Peters, was killed when his A-4E (BuNo 150017) took 37 mm flak hits over Do Son. Peters struggled to retain control as his Skyhawk lost fuel and finally caught fire. As he went feet wet, trying to get over water, the aircraft burst into flames and rolled inverted, diving for the sea below. Although Cdr Peters was seen to eject at low level, he was never recovered and was presumed to have drowned.

One of the lesser known 'Scooter' units, VA-216 deployed in *Hancock* as part of CVW-21. Two of its pilots received the Silver Star for action during the 1966 cruise. Lt C O Tolbert was on a mission in May and Cdr Carl Birdwell, the CO, received his award for a POL strike on 7 July. VA-216 lost several aircraft during the initial stages of the POL strikes.

Lt Cdr O F Baldwin was shot down on 21 May in A-4C BuNo 148474, but he was rescued. He would be shot down again barely six weeks later, on 4 July, in Skyhawk BuNo 149616, and again would be rescued. Lt(jg) Paul E Galanti was shot down on 17 June, flying A-4C BuNo 149528. He was captured and spent the next seven years as a PoW.

On 7 July, Lt Cdr William J Isenhour, also of VA-216, was part of the *Hancock* strike package. Heading for the POL area at Haiphong, his jet was hit by flak and began streaming smoke. Having to disconnect the hydraulic control system, Isenhour was forced to fly the little jet manually. However, the A-4's electrical system failed and the Skyhawk began to roll, forcing its pilot to eject. A Navy helicopter picked him up.

Fully laden with bombs, this A-4C (BuNo 147709) launches from *Ranger* in August 1966. The load, notably without an auxiliary fuel tank, suggests a mission against communist POL targets in North Vietnam. There is probably an A-3 or A-4 tanker waiting for this Skyhawk and, most likely, the carrier is fairly close to the North Vietnamese coast, thereby reducing the distance the strike aircraft must fly. BuNo 147709 was later hit by a SAM on 14 July 1967 while serving with VA-76 aboard 'Bonnie Dick'. The pilot, squadron CO Cdr (later RAdm) Robert B Fuller, made his attack run before ejecting and becoming a PoW

One of the most famous episodes involving an A-4 pilot during this period occurred on 23 July. Cdr Wynn F Foster, who had been the CAG's wingman the previous November when Cdr James Stockdale was shot down, was now CO of *Oriskany's* VA-163. He was leading a section of A-4Cs during an attack on POL facilities. It was Foster's 238th combat mission – he had flown 75 sorties in F9F Panthers during the Korean War as a member of VF-721 from USS *Kearsarge* (CV-33).

The A-4Es had launched at 0750 hrs and climbed to 12,000 ft for their brief flight to the target. Shortly after going feet dry, the section started its descent, quickly running into a barrage of flak bursts off to their right.

'I called the flak to my wingman's attention', Foster later wrote in an article for *Approach* magazine, 'and told him to keep jinking. A few seconds later I heard a loud "bang" followed by a "whoosh" and I felt a stinging sensation in my right elbow. I realised I had been hit and looked down at my right arm. The arm was missing from the elbow down and half my right forearm was laying on the starboard console.'

Cdr Foster's Skyhawk (BuNo 152100) had been hit by a 57 mm shell and shrapnel had severed his forearm. What followed was a classic story of pilot skill and determination as he turned back for his ship. His wingman, Lt(jg) Tom Spitzer, was on his first combat mission, having just checked into the squadron.

Cdr Foster took the stick with his left hand and headed back over the water. He called 'Mayday' over the radio and told Spitzer to keep jinking to avoid any unseen flak. Meanwhile, he saw his airspeed dropping. He dropped the nose slightly to reach 220 knots. Then he took stock of his situation. The burst had blown out most of his cockpit canopy, and the cockpit was littered with shrapnel and blood. The wind noise was terrible as he tried to communicate with his young wingman.

'My arm didn't hurt but I was bleeding quite badly. I momentarily considered trying to make it back to the ship but realised I would probably pass out before I got there. The nearest "friendly" was the SAR destroyer stationed about 30 miles from the coast-in point.'

As he descended to 2500 ft, Foster was flying on only 70 percent power. He pushed the throttle forward and the power spooled up, thereby relieving his fear that the flak had also hit the engine. He climbed back to 4000 ft. He and his wingman contacted the SAR destroyer USS *Reeves* to tell its crew that they were approaching from the southwest and were 15 miles away. There was no doubt that he would have to eject, and as he levelled at 3000 ft, Foster saw the small grey ship heading towards him.

By now, having lost so much blood and with shock setting in, Cdr Foster felt light-headed and was experiencing tunnel vision. He was three miles from the ship when he pulled the seat face curtain with his left hand. Fortunately, the ejection sequence went 'as advertised,' and he soon found himself suspended under the canopy, drifting toward the water.

'My oxygen mask was still on and my visor was down. I removed the oxygen mask and dropped it. I looked around. The view was beautiful – blue ocean, white clouds above and the destroyer steaming down below. The war seemed a million miles away.'

The destroyer sent a whaleboat to pick up the badly wounded aviator. Once aboard, Cdr Foster received initial medical treatment and was eventually transferred back to *Oriskany*. As the carrier was scheduled to

Cdr Wynn Foster poses by his Skyhawk in early 1966. His chequered helmet is a hallmark of VA-163 – the squadron he commanded when he was seriously injured during a POL strike on 23 July 1966

return to Cubi Point, in the Philippines, within a week, the medical staff decided to keep the VA-163 skipper on board instead of flying him off.

It was a case of déjà vu for Foster. He had taken command the previous November when VA-163's CO, Cdr Harry Jenkins, had been shot down. At one point Foster had been the XO, and within a few hours he was the CO. Now it was his turn to make a quick turnover. However, the senior officers of the wing and the captain of the ship, John Iarrobino, decided to delay the change of command until making port. It was the decent thing to do – let Cdr Foster retain his assignment as commanding officer, even though he could no longer lead from the cockpit. A week later, Cdr Ron Caldwell took over the squadron.

Wynn Foster began a long period of recuperation and therapy, fighting to remain on active duty. He received the Silver Star and the Purple Heart for the harrowing mission of 23 July. He also received the Distinguished Flying Cross (DFC) for leading a POL strike a few days before his life-changing sortie. Foster's request to remain on active duty was eventually approved and he retired in 1972 as a captain. Sadly, his wingman, Lt(jg) Tom Spitzer, died in the fire that struck *Oriskany* in the coming October.

'SAINTS' AND 'GHOSTRIDERS'

Oriskany's two A-4E squadrons are among the best known of the Vietnam-era carrier squadrons, and certainly had their share of top aviators and skilled leaders. Both units were established in September 1960, and their service was short as these things go. VA-163 made four war cruises before decommissioning in July 1971. VA-164, however, made seven combat deployments before it, too, disestablished in December 1975. Whereas long-lived units deployed with several carriers and flew a variety of aircraft, these two squadrons served aboard only two carriers – *Oriskany* and *Hancock* – and flew only the Skyhawk. Indeed, their story is, in large part, the story of the carrier air war in Vietnam.

VA-163 lost two COs within a year. Cdr Harry T Jenkins Jr was shot down on 13 November 1965 while on an armed reconnaissance mission just north of the DMZ. He spent the rest of the war as a PoW. As just related, his relief, Cdr Wynn Foster, was badly wounded barely eight months later and also had to relinquish command prematurely. Jenkins was a popular CO and was occasionally called 'CinCSaint V'.

These men were strong personalities and leaders. Cdr (later RAdm) Bryan W Compton Jr took over VA-163 on 10 July 1967, and a month later flew a mission for which he received the Navy Cross.

VA-164 was more fortunate and did not lose a CO during the war. It did lose jets and pilots, however.

During the 1965 cruise, VA-163 pilots averaged 154 missions each, totalling 2793 sorties and 6445 flight hours. Some 250 decorations were earned, with Lt(jg) Charles Stender garnering four DFCs, 13

Two VA-164 A-4Es tote what is probably the heaviest bomb load the diminutive A-4 could handle – a centreline-mounted Mk 84 2000-lb bomb, two Mk 83 1000-lb bombs and two Mk 82 500-lb bombs. When carrying 5000 lbs of ordnance, the A-4 had to make do without the usual one or two auxiliary fuel tanks. This photograph shows the earliest version of the *LADY JESSIE* marking, with 'AH 407' (BuNo 151180) being flown here by the pilot who started the tradition, Lt Cdr Richard C Perry

Air Medals and a Navy Commendation Medal – an impressive collection for such a junior pilot.

VA-164 lost nugget pilot Ens George P McSwain on 28 July 1966 when his A-4E (BuNo 152077) was downed by a SAM after he had fired a Shrike at the missile battery. He was on an *Iron Hand* anti-SAM mission at the time, and the SA-2 exploded nearby, sending his jet out of control. McSwain ejected and was captured, spending the next six-and-a-half years as a PoW. 'Ghostrider' pilot Lt(jg) Don Ewoldt died in a flight mishap the following day, flying into the water during a tanker hop.

A second VA-164 flight mishap on 25 August took the life of Lt(jg) William H Bullard, who crashed soon after launch for a night mission. Whether in combat or operating around the ship, this period proved how dangerous carrier aviation could be.

FIRE ON THE 'O-BOAT'

The threat of fire stalks every ship that ever put to sea. In military vessels, training to fight fires of all types is part of the daily regimen. All crewmen, officers and enlisted, ship's company and air wing members, are expected to at least know how to respond to a fire and contribute to its control and extinguishing. Crews are constantly admonished about safety in general, and particular that pertaining to fires. However, there are always a few that do not get the word or choose to ignore their training. When two young seamen forgot their training and accidentally started a fire at 0700 hrs on 26 October, they initiated a massive tragedy that ultimately resulted in the deaths of 44 shipmates.

The flames burned through four levels, reaching the officer staterooms and trapping many pilots in their bunks or in smoke-darkened passageways. Some died in their beds, others as they tried desperately to escape. Twenty-four pilots were killed in total, including newly installed CAG Cdr Rodney B Carter, who had been the leader of CVW-16 for

Oriskany crewmen cluster amid four burnt and blackened A-4Es of VA-163 and VA-164 after the devastating fire on 26 October 1966. This quartet of jets had been hastily evacuated from hangar bay one up to the flightdeck during the fire. The A-4 on the right is missing its canopy following the partial firing of its ejection seat during the height of the blaze. Three Skyhawks suffered varying degrees of damage and one was destroyed (VA-163's BuNo 151075) in the conflagration, which also killed 36 officers (24 of whom were Naval Aviators) and eight enlisted men

only two weeks. He was preparing to brief for a mission with VA-163 at the time. Four members of VA-163 and four from VA-164 died.

Unfortunately, the *Oriskany* fire was only the first of four major conflagrations that would strike carriers during the Vietnam War.

'ROSIE'S' WAR

Although it had been in service since shortly after the end of World War 2, USS *Franklin D Roosevelt* (CVA-42) had never seen combat. It had spent most of its time plying the Atlantic and Mediterranean. However, the increasing tempo of Vietnam operations showed that the number of ships normally dedicated to the Pacific Fleet was not enough, or that those carriers assigned to Task Force 77 (CTF 77) were in need of rest and repair. Therefore, the Atlantic Fleet was occasionally tasked to provide carriers to augment the war effort.

'FDR', or 'Rosie' as she was sometimes known, and her CVW-1 made a one-time combat cruise commencing on 21 June 1966. Among the air wing squadrons were two A-4E units, VA-12 and VA-72, and one A-4C squadron, VA-172. VA-72, normally assigned to CVW-7 aboard *Independence*, had replaced VA-15, which had been flying the veteran A-1 Skyraider and was transitioning to the equally elderly A-4B.

CVW-1 flew its first missions on 10 August. 'Rosie' stayed on the line for a month, then began a port visit to Yokosuka, Japan. The second line period did not start well, as the carrier's No 1 screw lost a blade, requiring the ship to head back to Yokosuka for repairs. 'FDR' eventually returned to *Yankee Station* on 20 October.

During the first line period 'Rosie's' squadrons had seen much action, with VA-72 losing two jets in two days. On 21 August, Lt A R Carpenter was flying an armed reconnaissance mission near Thanh Hoa. His section attacked a railway target, and as he began his second run, Carpenter heard an explosion and turned for the sea. However, the A-4E (BuNo 151109) burst into flames and he ejected to be picked up by a Navy helicopter.

Lt Carpenter was not so fortunate three months later when he was shot down by flak while attacking a SAM site on 1 November. This time he was captured, despite an intense SAR effort that saw the rescue helicopter and its escorting A-4s all suffer damage from enemy ground fire.

The day after Carpenter's 21 August mission, fellow 'Blue Hawk' pilot Lt Ken Craig had the frustrating experience of running into debris from the salvo of 2.75-in rockets he had just fired at a junk. The engine of his A-4E (BuNo 149992) ingested parts of the rockets, which quickly resulted in a loss of power and control – there is conjecture that rocket debris may have also downed Carpenter's jet the previous day. Craig ejected and was picked up by a Navy helicopter.

During 'FDR's' second line period, on 20 October, VA-172's Lt(jg) Fred Purrington was shot down while on one of the innumerable armed reconnaissance missions that filled aviators' flight logs during the war. It was a catchall phrase that included everything from individual attacks on targets of opportunity to scouting out activity on roads and waterways. Hit by flak, his A-4C (BuNo 147775) was badly damaged and its cockpit filled with smoke, at which point Purrington ejected into captivity.

Two other VA-172 aviators were killed in action, both on 2 December. CO, Cdr Bruce A Nystrom, was the section leader for a night armed reconnaissance with Ens Paul L Worrell. Fifty miles south of Haiphong, the two A-4Cs were tracked by a SAM battery. Worrell told his leader and Nystrom in turn called for evasive manoeuvres. However, other crews in the area saw two SAM launches, followed by flashes. The Skyhawks had disappeared. Ens Worrell's remains were returned by the North Vietnamese in 1985.

Two A-4Es from VA-12 were involved in a mid-air collision on 12 November, and although they were returning from a mission, the loss of the two pilots – squadron CO Cdr Robert C Frosio and Lt(jg) James G Jones – was not as a direct result of combat.

'Rosie's' last A-4 combat loss came on 14 December, just before the carrier prepared to rotate home. Lt Claude D Wilson of VA-72 was on an *Iron Hand* mission, which was part of a larger raid. He had become separated from his flight lead and was hit by a SAM. Reportedly, the young pilot kept flying level following this first impact, instead of jinking, although he might have been injured. A second missile quickly found his A-4E (BuNo 151068) and the Skyhawk disintegrated. The North Vietnamese returned Wilson's remains in 1989.

After 33 days on the line, 'FDR' headed for home on 27 December. After calling at Hong Kong, Subic Bay and Cape Town, in South Africa, the vessel returned to Mayport, Florida, on 21 February 1967. It had been a long and eventful cruise. *Roosevelt* would not be the only 'ringer' to make an early war cruise.

It had been a dozen years since the Korean War, and even though the Navy had been deploying carriers, and their air wings, throughout the world with appropriate training cycles and new aircraft, there was nothing like the shock of real combat to point out the system's faults.

Besides the realisation that it was facing another oriental enemy whose take on life was drastically different, the Navy (as well as the rest of the US military) quickly found that it did not have sufficient assets to easily rotate units in and out of the combat area. After Korea, the Navy thought it had the luxury of fielding different types of carriers that could specialise in such things as ASW or the more traditional role of attack and power projection. The smaller, older *Essex*-class 27C conversions were given the ASW role, embarking air wings made up of helicopters with specialised sonar gear, as well as S-2 Trackers – twin-engined, highly capable aircraft from Grumman that carried the latest radar and appropriate weapons for hunting submarines.

A few of the 27Cs – *Hancock*, *Ticonderoga*, *Oriskany* and *Bon Homme Richard* – kept their CVA attack role, but others such as *Yorktown*, *Kearsarge*, *Intrepid* and, much later, *Shangri-la*, morphed into hybrids, sending their ASW aircraft to the beach and taking on modified wings of A-4s and F-8s, all to augment the hard-pressed traditional ships.

Signalling all is ready, a crewman gets out of the way before a VA-12 A-4C launches from 'FDR' on 6 September 1966. The 'Charlie' carries two 300-gallon fuel tanks and all its bombs on the centreline multiple ejection racks. Note the striking 'Kiss of Death' squadron insignia on the fuselage (*Neal Crowe*)

Ranger ordnancemen position a Mk 84 2000-lb bomb in front of an A-4C from VA-146. Note the nose of an RA-5C (Modex 125) from RVAH-9 parked between the two 'Blue Diamonds' jets

Kearsarge and *Yorktown* probably had the strangest mix, as their CVSG groups included detachments of A-4s nestled within the mix of S-2s and SH-3s. *Yorktown* even had a det of A-4Cs from VMA-223 during its 1965 deployment – a Marine Corps attack squadron sailing with a Navy ASW wing! There was also a dedicated 'fighter' squadron – VSF-3 – flying A-4Bs.

Intrepid was probably the most successful of these modified carriers, making three war cruises from 1965 to 1968. With its ASW designation CVS temporarily changed to CVA, 'the Fighting I' made its first combat deployment in the thick of the opening months of the POL campaign. CVW-10's complement included VA-15 and VA-95, both flying elderly A-4Bs.

The next cruise had an enlarged wing, with VA-15 and VA-34 now operating A-4Cs, and VSF-3 (Anti-Submarine Fighter Squadron Three) using 'Bravos' to provide dedicated fighter cover, even though there was a detachment of F-8Cs from VF-111 embarked. This was a busy cruise in which three A-4Bs and nine A-4Cs were lost, although not all of them in combat.

Intrepid's third and final combat deployment was probably the most intense. CVW-10 now included three attack A-4 squadrons – VA-36 and VA-66 flying 'Charlies' and VA-106 flying 'Echoes'.

Cdr Ken Burrows had an unusually long tour as CAG. He took command of CVSG-10 on 23 June 1966 and remained until 12 January 1968. The normal tour was about a year. He had flown fighters in Korea then commanded VA-172, flying A-4s. During two combat deployments aboard *Intrepid*, he flew 135 missions. After several other assignments, he retired as a captain. He recalled his time as CAG;

'Both my CAG cruises were with an all-attack air wing. The wing was well equipped and trained for the mission of supporting our ground forces in South Vietnam.'

Burrows, however, realised the wing needed more training if it was to venture into North Vietnam. He ordered more training flights that concentrated on air-to-air and avoiding SAMs. Fuel management and using the right ECM gear were also primary concerns.

'Strict radio discipline was mandatory in combat, and it was my custom to have strike leaders do all the talking. All Alpha strikes were led either by myself or a squadron commander.'

By year end, it was obvious that there remained a lot of work to do to bring the war to a favourable conclusion. Ground action was furious, and the jungles below were turning into meat grinders. Although Naval Aviators, and their compatriots ashore, had tried to halt the constant flow of men and supplies south, the results were less than satisfactory and the price was becoming increasingly steep. 1967 would be no better.

HEAVIEST ACTION AND GREATEST LOSSES

As 1967 began, it was evident that the interdiction campaign was causing Hanoi extreme hardships. The entire population of North Vietnam had been mobilised to support the war effort. Senior military officials tried to breathe new life into their offensive. Adm U S G Sharp, Commander-in-Chief, Pacific, said, 'There were six basic target systems in North Vietnam – electric power, war supporting industry, transportation support facilities, military complexes, petroleum storage and air defence'. He wanted Washington to relax the restrictions on bombing the inner portions of Hanoi.

Most military commanders agreed that even with strikes on important industrial areas outside the city, until major civilian centres of population were affected, the communists would never come to the peace table. Meanwhile, the men in the cockpits watched their comrades dive into the barrages of heavy-calibre flak and SAMs over Hanoi and Haiphong, or over the jungle nests of 23 mm and 37 mm flak guns, and die or eject into unknown captivity.

For the first few weeks of 1967, the carrier air wings flew road recces or struck railway targets. Several A-4s were lost and their pilots killed or captured, beginning on 4 January when VA-22's Lt(jg) J M Hays, participating in a strike on Haiphong, had his jet catch fire. He made it over the water, punched out and was rescued by a waiting helicopter.

The following day, VA-192's Lt Cdr Richard A Stratton, and his flight, attacked a ferry south of Thanh Hoa. Flying into debris from the salvo of rockets that he had just fired, Stratton damaged his A-4E's engine to the point where he had to eject over land. He was soon captured. Stratton was to gain a painful measure of fame during his incarceration when he was shown bowing to his captors for a foreign film crew. But his indomitable spirit eventually came through and the value of his act was destroyed.

Stratton had been called at 0130 hrs on 5 January from his bunk by VA-192's operations officer, Lt Cdr Mike Estocin (about whom much more will be heard in the coming pages). The latter asked Stratton, who was the squadron maintenance officer, if he would take his scheduled weather reconnaissance hop because Estocin had to go to a meeting with the CAG. Stratton accommodated his friend and agreed.

Ironically, Stratton would fly VA-192's 'CAG bird', 'NM 400' (BuNo 151136), on this fateful mission. Each squadron had a designated aircraft using '00' for part of the side number, or modex. The aeroplane was 'assigned' to the air wing commander and displayed his name below the cockpit canopy. This aircraft also normally carried, in some form on the tail, all the colours of the wing that indicated the individual squadrons.

After flying the scheduled route, the two A-4 pilots spotted a river junk and fired some of their rockets at it. Next, Stratton went after a few bridge sections he had seen. 'The only ordnance I had left were Aero-7D rocket packs, so I unloaded them on the bridge sections', he later recalled.

The rocket pack had not been the most dependable item in the weapons line-up. The rocket fins that were supposed to unfold and stabilise the little missiles did not work that day, resulting in some of the rockets colliding with each other and exploding. These showered Stratton's A-4 with shrapnel, which his engine quickly ingested.

'At 2200 ft and 220 knots, the engine gave up and exploded. In the process it blew off the tail, and my ever-loving A-4 flying machine had all the flight characteristics of a free-falling safe.'

Just before he ejected, he thought of his family, especially his wife's admonishment not to die and leave her alone with their three children. For the next 2251 days he had plenty of time to think of an answer when he next saw them.

Lt(jg) Michael P Cronin became the next Skyhawk PoW on 13 January when his A-4E (BuNo 151158) took a hit from North Vietnamese flak south of Thanh Hoa. The VA-23 aviator was finally able to eject from his burning aircraft after being pinned in the cockpit by the G forces as the stricken Skyhawk broke apart. Although Cronin landed offshore, a strong wind pushed him toward the shore, and capture.

Three other Navy 'Scooters' were lost by the end of the month, one each from VA-56, VA-23, and VA-112.

The latter unit was one of two 'Charlie' squadrons deployed in *Kitty Hawk* in 1967. Perhaps not one of the more well-known A-4 squadrons, the 'Broncos' did see considerable action during the mid-war period, flying A-4Cs until the unit was disestablished in October 1969, following a final combat deployment aboard *Ticonderoga*.

Cdr Charles H Brown was the XO, and he recalled one night mission on 20 January 1967, shortly after the start of the carrier's first line period. Launched on a night interdiction, his section was to find and attack any trucks bringing supplies into South Vietnam along Route One – one of the major routes just a few miles in from the coast that ran from North Vietnam to South Vietnam.

The A-4s were soon into the clouds that characterised the monsoon period of the year. The ship was fairly close to the coast, and Brown took his section across the land, turning off their lights to make them less visible from the ground. The conditions soon made keeping track of the trail difficult, but the 'Bronco' pilots pressed on. Occasionally, the two aviators could see bursts of light flak sent up at other aircraft – they were too far away to be meant for the VA-112 section. Still, to know the enemy was awake and alert brought the usual caution.

As Cdr Brown later wrote, 'The 23 mm weapon at night really attracted my attention. That gun's rate of fire was so fast that the stream of bullets, always with tracers at night, looked like burning water from a fire hose. At the end of the stream's trajectory, it sort of petered out, tracers dropping like a fancy fireworks burst'.

Reaching the northern end of their patrol area, the two A-4s turned back toward Route One. Soon, they saw what must have been lights from moving trucks headed south. Checking that their 20 mm cannon and bombs were armed, Brown made the first attack, strafing the targets with his wing guns. His wingman, Lt(jg) Jerry Hogan (in A-4C BuNo 145144), watched, replying to the XO's call that he had discovered some worthwhile targets. Hogan began his run.

Cdr Brown made a second pass then pulled off and waited to hear from his junior pilot. The minutes passed, but Hogan did not respond to his leader's calls. The flares that Brown had dropped were gone, and the area was again in darkness. There had been no explosion to show that an aeroplane had crashed. Brown fired off his remaining flares but saw nothing of his wingman.

A section of F-4s joined the search, but all three aircraft soon needed fuel, and Brown called up an orbiting KA-3 tanker, which obliged. After refuelling, Brown recovered back aboard. Lt(jg) Hogan did not return, and it could only be surmised that he had gone in, perhaps misjudging his dive in the darkness. It was, unfortunately, not an uncommon event that a pilot, especially a younger, less experienced one, would develop target fixation or be distracted at the wrong time.

THE WAR HEATS UP

On 24 February 1967 some of the gloves came off. On that date, an Alpha strike against the important MiG base at Kep, north-east of Hanoi, signalled that the US was going to hit these heretofore protected sanctuaries. *Kitty Hawk* sent VA-112 and VA-144 on the strike. The day before, A-6s had mined the Song Ca and South Giang rivers, thereby also lifting restrictions from this important option. In the coming weeks other areas were also mined. However, the vital ports of Haiphong, Hon Gai and Cam Pha remained protected.

'Tico' lost A-4E BuNo 151108 from VA-192 on 12 March, its pilot being squadron XO, Cdr Ernest M Moore. An experienced attack pilot with more than 90 missions under his belt, including several *Iron Hand* sorties, Moore was shot down by a SAM. The XO ejected from his burning aircraft and was immediately captured.

VA-112's Lt Alexander J Palenscar was lost on 27 March during an attack on a bridge northwest of Vinh. His flight of four A-4Cs bombed the span, and Lt Palenscar was the tail end Charlie (in BuNo 148519), bringing up the rear. His last radio call was that he was off target and coming to rejoin the group. However, he was not seen again and presumed killed.

'TICO'S' TIME

As new planning and new targets were added to the daily mix, each ship and its air wing was often pushed to the limits of human endurance and capability. The 27C-class carrier *Ticonderoga* was in the thick of things for the month of April. On 7 April, Cdr Charles E Hathaway, CO of VA-195, flew his 281st combat mission. He had been awarded a DFC on 5 February, and today he led a section of A-4Cs against a truck park. After dropping their bombs, they came around to strafe with their cannon. It was at this point that Hathaway felt his jet shudder from ground fire. The

Cdr Charles E Hathaway strides across 'Tico's' flightdeck in mid-February 1967. He had received the DFC on the 5th of that month. The CO of VA-195, Hathaway ejected on 7 April on his 281st mission. He eventually accumulated 304 combat sorties, which was the highest number for a Naval Aviator at that stage in the war

oxygen system had been struck, and his wingman quickly warned him that he could see flames trailing some 200 ft behind the stricken Skyhawk.

Hathaway hung on until he went feet wet, then ejected. A helicopter retrieved him and he was back aboard 'Tico' to eventually fly 23 more missions for a total of 304 – for a time the highest of any Naval Aviator in South-east Asia. His XO, Cdr Sam Chessman, who eventually relieved Hathaway, passed him with 306. However, those numbers would be only half the number of sorties accrued by the eventual leader.

10 April brought another aircraft loss for 'Tico' when VA-192's Lt Cdr George W Shattuck took a hit from flak while on an armed reconnaissance mission north of Vinh. With reduced power and control, he could not take on fuel from a tanker to return to the carrier. He had to eject when the engine flamed out due to fuel starvation. Shattuck was retrieved by a helicopter.

The 'Golden Dragons' of VA-192 lost yet another aircraft on 25 April. Lt Cdr F J Almberg was on an *Iron Hand* flight north of Haiphong when he was targeted by the SAM battery he had just attacked with a Shrike anti-radiation missile. The site fired one missile, which exploded nearby without harming his jet. However, a second SA-2's explosion was closer and the debris hit the A-4E, fatally damaging its hydraulic system.

A Skyhawk pilot could disconnect the hydraulic control system and fly the aircraft manually. Several pilots used this feature to retain control of their wounded A-4s. If they were not able to recover aboard their ship, at least they could fly out over the water to eject and be rescued by orbiting helicopters. Lt Cdr Almberg headed for the SAR destroyer. Finally, he lost all control and ejected. The duty SAR helicopter retrieved him.

ONE BUSY DAY FOR THE 'DRAGONS'

VA-192 saw yet more action on the 26th, when besides losing two aircraft and one aviator, the day's missions would see two high-level medals eventually awarded, including the only Medal of Honor for aerial action to go to a fixed-wing carrier pilot during the Vietnam War.

Lt(jg) John W Cain launched as part of a POL raid in A-4E BuNo 152076 – the squadron's CAG bird, 'NM 200', call sign 'Jury 200'. Making his attack run, Cain's A-4 was hit and the cockpit filled with smoke. The young aviator continued his attack but the A-4 began to roll, and he disconnected the hydraulics so as to fly on manual. The procedure did not work, however, and at 2000 ft, barely making 205 knots, Cain ejected and came down just offshore, 15 miles south of Haiphong near the harbour entrance.

Cain lost his personal survival radio during the ejection, and thus could not call for help. A full-blown SAR developed, complete with orbiting F-8s and A-1s providing much-needed CAP services. Eventually, there were 20 aircraft involved – 19 were fixed-wing, while the 20th was an SH-3A from HS-2, normally part of *Hornet's* air group, pulling SAR duty aboard the guided missile destroyer USS *Mahan* (DLG-11).

Lt Steve Millikin and his crew heard the call that an aviator was down in the harbour. Orbiting as the strike group had passed over, the crew of 'Chink 69' had been amusing themselves by indulging in Tonkin Gulf 'plinking' – shooting at debris in the harbour. Millikin firewalled the throttles, which for an SH-3 meant steaming ahead at 125 knots. Cain was only 250 yards offshore of a small island where there were enemy troops watching, waiting.

Soon, the troops began firing at Cain as he drifted in the water. He had decided to not get into his personal life raft because it would have provided too much of a target. His prospects looked bleak, but then he heard the beat of helicopter rotors as 'Chink 69' approached. Lt Millikin told Petty Officer Peter Sorokin to lower the rescue horse collar. The fire from the shore increased as Millikin entered a hover over Cain, and he could see the water erupt into geysers as the rounds came perilously close. At first he thought the shots were coming from Navy A-1s, but Millikin soon realised they were North Vietnamese mortar rounds.

Petty Officer Charles Sather returned fire with his door-mounted machine gun, while the co-pilot, Lt(jg) Tom Pettis, stuck a submachine gun out his window and added to the small barrage coming from the struggling H-3. The engagement intensified, but finally Cain was in the sling, and as he was still on his way up, Millikin turned the H-3 about and got out as quickly as he could. As he chanced a glance back to the island, he watched an A-4 drop four bombs on the enemy. Millikin smiled as a part of the island seemed to slide into the harbour.

The exhausted crew and their young survivor made it back to *Mahan*, and later that day they delivered Lt(jg) Cain to *Ticonderoga*. Lt Millikin received the Silver Star, Lt(jg) Pettis the DFC and the two enlisted crewmen Air Medals for their efforts. Unfortunately, 'Chink 69' and Lt(jg) Pettis were lost at sea several weeks later. Steve Millikin retired as a captain and subsequently became well known as editor of *The Hook*, the highly regarded quarterly magazine of the Tailhook Association.

MEDAL OF HONOR FROM TURTLE CREEK

Just 19 pilots received the Medal of Honor during the eight-year war in Vietnam. USAF aircrew received ten medals, Army aviators got five and the Marine Corps just one. Naval Aviators were awarded two medals for aerial action, with a third going to Cdr James Stockdale for his service while a PoW in Hanoi. Skyhawk pilot Lt Cdr Michael J Estocin was the only Naval Aviator to receive the award for his bravery in the cockpit of a fast jet.

Mike Estocin was a native of Turtle Creek, Pennsylvania, south-east of Pittsburgh. Born in 1931, he graduated from Slippery Rock State College before joining the Navy. A serious, focused individual, but with a sense of humour, Estocin had always wanted to fly. An avid reader, he was also interested in the law and the stock market. He would earn the Medal of Honor one day before his 36th birthday, which he would never see.

One of VA-192's most respected officers, Estocin was an *Iron Hand* specialist who often flew these extremely dangerous missions, taking his A-4 right down the throat of an SA-2 battery before releasing his Shrike missile. This weapon was not as dependable as the missiles of some 40 years later. Often, the *Iron Hand* pilot would have to shoot a second, or even a third Shrike to accomplish his task, which was to kill the SA-2 and its attendant support vehicles and crew.

By April 1967, tactics and equipment to fight the increasing number of SAMs were constantly evolving, and it took a special breed of aviator to fly the mission. Such a man was Mike Estocin.

VA-192's Lt Cdr Michael Estocin received the only Medal of Honor given to a Naval Aviator for action flying a fixed-wing aircraft during the war

Actually, his Medal of Honor was given to him as a result of *two* missions. On 20 April, Estocin had accompanied a strike group hitting two North Vietnamese thermal powerplants near Haiphong. The three A-4s successfully attacked three missile sites. However, Estocin's Skyhawk sustained severe damage from a SAM detonating during the second attack. Undeterred, after checking his aircraft for control problems, he returned to attack the third site.

Regrouping, the three Skyhawks flew back over the water to find a tanker. Estocin's A-4 was streaming jet fuel, and with an estimated five minutes of gas left, he found the orbiting KA-3 tanker and plugged in. But his jet was losing fuel faster than he could take it, and so as would occasionally happen during the war, the big 'Whale' towed the struggling little attack bomber back to its carrier. Three miles behind the ship, and with enough fuel for only one try, Estocin unplugged and drove his aircraft toward *Ticonderoga*. Listening to the calls from the LSO, he flopped onto the deck and waited as the fire-fighter crew smothered the burning A-4 with foam. It was the stuff movies are made of, and Mike Estocin had more to come six days later.

On 26 April, he was scheduled to fly the big POL strike that saw Lt(jg) John Cain's dramatic rescue. As the main force swept in across the tank farm, Mike and his F-8 escort held off in orbit, watching for any signs of SAMs. Finally, the radar warning receivers lit up – the SAM batteries were active. As the ship-based radar controller called that the strike force was heading for home, Estocin and F-8 pilot Lt Cdr John Nichols (who would get a MiG-17 kill a year later) scanned the skies for missiles.

Suddenly, they both caught the flash of a launch some 12,000 ft below. Nichols waited for the A-4 pilot to turn, but Estocin kept boring in, intent on confronting the oncoming SAM. However it happened – perhaps Estocin had misjudged the missile's distance – the SAM exploded near the A-4, which began to spin and burn, shedding pieces of debris. Somehow, the pilot righted the stricken little jet some 2000 ft above the ground and Nichols slid in for a closer look to check on his friend. Both jets were flying at just 160 knots, which was barely above stalling speed.

The F-8 pilot called to the man he could see slumped over in the shattered A-4 cockpit, but there was no response. The Skyhawk was in shreds, staggering through the air. Finally, it rolled inverted and the two Shrike missiles launched themselves as the A-4 dived into the ground. There was nothing Nichols could do. He called the incoming rescue forces, which held offshore as the F-8 went feet wet back to the ship.

At first, CVW-19 wrote a citation for the Navy Cross (Estocin had also received the Silver Star shortly before his last mission), but the senior admirals wanted something more and sent the write-up back, saying they would support 'an upgrade'. There was only one 'upgrade' higher than the Navy Cross, and finally, in 1978, Capt Estocin's family (he had since been promoted posthumously) received his Medal of Honor.

At the time of his last mission, Estocin's ultimate fate was not initially confirmed, and there were confusing reports that he had, in fact, ejected and survived, and might be a PoW. These rumours made it hard for his family to put him to rest, but Mike Estocin had died with his aeroplane. His dedication to duty and his skill in the face of incredible enemy opposition are why he truly deserved to be remembered by the Medal of

Honor. In 1981 the Navy named a newly commissioned frigate (FFG-15) for him, and it served until 2003, when it was decommissioned and sold to Turkey.

TOUGH LITTLE 'SCOOTER'

On 25 April, Lt(jg) Al Crebo of VA-212, aboard *Bon Homme Richard*, was part of a raid against an ammunition depot near Haiphong. After approaching the target and climbing to 8000 ft to begin his delivery dive, Crebo had an SA-2 explode nearby;

'I was assigned to the afternoon strike. There was considerable consternation in the air group, since the morning strike group had sustained significant battle damage, including the loss of an A-4C from VA-76. Our good friend Charlie Stackhouse had been shot down by a MiG-17, and we didn't know if he had survived the ejection. Fortunately, as we found out later, he was alive and had been taken prisoner.

'Our target for the last strike of the day was the Kien An ammunition depot near Cat Bi airfield, on the southern edge of Haiphong. I had an uneasy feeling about this strike for a number of reasons. The question of strike tactics was the subject of a great deal of discussion at that early stage of the cruise. Some people thought we should coast in low at about 3500 ft, then climb to 7000 ft over the target for the attack. Such an approach would allow us to stay out of the SAM envelope for as long as possible. The problem with this tactic was that aircraft heavily loaded with ordnance would be over the target at low speed. We therefore discarded this approach in favour of a high coast-in from about 14,000 ft, with a gradual acceleration and decreasing altitude to arrive in the target area at high speed.

'We never made repeated runs over the same target. High, steep, fast, and once proved much more effective. However, it was early in the cruise, and we had not reached that level of sophistication.

'Another concern was the fact that there were two strike groups ahead of us in the general area. There would be no element of surprise. Also, the second strike group would be on its way out while we were on our way in.'

Crebo's group consisted of six A-4Es from VA-212 – a four-aeroplane division and a section of two. VA-76 contributed four A-4Cs as flak suppressors. Two more VA-212 'Scooters' went along as *Iron Hand* aircraft, carrying Shrikes. Four F-8Es from VF-211 would also furnish flak suppression, while four F-8Cs from VF-24 would fly TARCAP, guarding against MiG interceptors. VA-215 Skyraiders were tasked with SARCAP duties to protect downed pilots. There were KA-3 tankers and RF-8s along as well. It was a big strike.

Although Lt(jg) Crebo was a junior pilot, and was assigned the number six slot, he had considerable A-4 time, having made a previous Med cruise with VA-64 aboard the newly commissioned USS *America* (CVA-66).

Coasting in, the strikers began receiving SAM warnings from the Air Force EC-121 orbiting off shore. The code word 'Hallmark', meaning SAMs, flooded the airwaves. Inside their cockpits, the A-4 pilots also heard the warble of their ALQ-51s – devices that detected the fire-control radar of the SAM launch battery. Flak was also beginning to appear. Grey and black puffs of 37 mm and 85 mm AAA dotted the sky. It was going to be a rough delivery.

Not for the superstitious! Lt(jg) Al Crebo has his photograph taken before boarding 'NP 225' on 25 April 1967. Less than two hours later he was fighting to keep his mangled A-4 in the air (*PH3 M H Flannery, via Alan R Crebo*)

The ALQ-51 was giving off a high-pitch warble and its red SAM light was also glowing. The Shrike jets and TARCAP detached and climbed to 20,000 ft. The attack plan was to roll in to the east and then be on course for the run-out back to the Gulf of Tonkin. Crebo recalled;

'Because of the climb we were at a very low speed over the target. It seemed like we were just hanging there for an eternity below 250 knots. I was number six on the roll-in, and when my jet was in a 90-degree bank, I was hit by a SAM coming from the west on the blind side. It felt like a moderately severe automobile accident. I was not surprised that I was hit because we were hanging over the target, exposed. I was also mildly angry with myself and the enemy.

'The first thing that happened was that another missile passed by a few yards off the starboard side of my aircraft. SAMs were proximity-fused, and were supposed to detonate when they came near an aircraft. Had that missile blown up, it would have ruined the rest of my day. The fact that the SAM did not detonate close to me was pure luck. The missile finally blew up ahead of me in a huge puff of orange smoke.

'At this point, virtually all the warning lights were on, including the fire-warning light. The A-4 was on fire. There was smoke coming out of my oxygen mask. When that second SAM detonated, I thought, "So that's what a SAM smells like when it goes off". After dismissing that ridiculous thought, I realised I was smelling smoke and tore off one of the mask fittings from my helmet.

'I was still hanging over the target. I was thinking first and foremost about escape. I knew the best way to convert altitude to airspeed was to dive. I did have a good view of the target and could see the other A-4s completing their runs. Out of revenge and self-preservation, I decided to attack on my way out to the water.

'Just after I had delivered my weapons in a rather steep run, the aeroplane became uncontrollable and rolled beyond 90 degrees to about 135 degrees of bank – I had lost hydraulics. I thought I was a dead man! I wondered what hitting the ground at this speed would feel like. I pulled the manual flight-control disconnect handle, and with considerable effort, I rolled wings level and pulled out of the dive.'

Lt(jg) Crebo heads his mortally wounded Skyhawk towards his carrier. Part of the large Alpha strike on the Haiphong Ammunition Depot on 25 April, Crebo's A-4E (BuNo 151102) was damaged by a SAM, losing most of its vertical tail and various fuselage panels and systems. Crebo could only lower his nose gear and arresting hook, making a safe recovery aboard ship impossible. He ejected close to the carrier and was retrieved by helicopter. After a medical check, Crebo was back on the flight schedule the following day! He received the Silver Star and Purple Heart for this harrowing mission (*via Alan R Crebo*)

Crebo was now at low altitude as he headed for the gulf. Several of his squadronmates joined on him as he struggled to make the relative safety of the water. They stared in disbelief at the battered A-4. It was trailing fuel and its rudder was gone, as were several fuselage panels. Later, Crebo learned that his horizontal stabilisers were skewed several degrees out of alignment – no wonder his Skyhawk was having trouble staying straight and level. When he tried to extend his gear and hook, only the hook and nose gear came down. Without his main gear, the option of trapping back aboard CVA-31 was gone. Ejection was now the only choice.

As Crebo tried to reach 10,000 ft, the engine finally ran out of fuel, or perhaps seized, at 6000 ft. Nose heavy, the Skyhawk dived for the water, making it impossible for Crebo to reach his face curtain to eject. He went for the secondary handle between his legs – a feature of most ejection seats, and included for just such a situation.

Crebo was rescued after only four minutes in the water, and incredibly was back on flight status the next day! He received the Silver Star for this mission. Al Crebo completed his tour with more than 200 missions to his credit. Leaving the Navy, he finished his medical training and became an ophthalmologic surgeon. The photographs of his flight out of North Vietnam became some of the classic images of the air war.

Lt(jg) Stephen Gray was another junior aviator in VA-212 that day. He related more of the overall mission, especially the ordeal of the squadron XO, Cdr Marvin M Quaid, who would assume command in May when Cdr Homer Smith was killed. This day, Quaid's A-4 had also taken a SAM hit. As the most junior aviator, Gray was flying on the XO's wing, and he had a ringside seat for what happened;

'"'Eagle Two's' got a SAM light", I bleated over the radio. The climb to 7000 ft seemed to take forever! I was relieved when Quaid finally rolled over and started the run. Anxious to get the nose into the dive and avoid the SAM, whose whereabouts I didn't know, I pulled inside Quaid's turn and ended up damn near in parade position on him, nearly abeam. We were supposed to separate far enough to make individual runs at the target and wheel around past lead's run-in line to avoid eating the flak that missed him.

'Frantically scanning for the target, I finally spotted it – low buildings, and I placed my pipper on the first row. At 4000 ft I stabbed the bomb pickle four times, feeling the little aeroplane buck and jump as the bombs came off. With the onset of Gs, I pulled up screaming against the bladder of my G-suit, with my left hand on the max G-suit inflate button, all the while trying to keep the XO's aeroplane in the small spot of vision that I had left.

'Suddenly, from right to left, a bright orange flash. Quaid's jet disappeared in the fireball, and there, directly on my nose, spun the still-burning rocket motor of the SAM. In reflex, I yanked back on the stick to miss the motor and flashed through the smoke and debris field from the explosion. Quaid's A-4 was a dim silhouette in a cloud of fuel and hydraulic vapour streaming from many holes in the wings and fuselage.

'"'Eagle Lead', you're hit! Head for the beach!" My call got no response. I added power and pulled alongside the XO. His jet was steadily losing speed and altitude, and he seemed to be slumped forward in the cockpit. "Oh shit", I thought, "He's dead!"'

Lt Stephen Gray rests his hand on a Zuni rocket pod slung under the starboard wing of his Skyhawk during the 1967 cruise

The two A-4s sped over a big flak site near the mouth of Haiphong harbour, and six guns – either heavy 85 mm or 100 mm weapons – threw up a curtain of fire. The bright yellow balls of flame bracketed the jets, and the radio was alive with calls. Finally, Gray heard a call from Cdr Quaid.

'"Eagle Six", I'm hit, and I'm losing control!'

Gray watched as the ram air turbine (RAT) came out from the right side of Quaid's aircraft. Hopefully, it would provide emergency electrical power for the stricken A-4.

'"Eagle Lead", do you know you're hit?' Gray made the incredible call, to which the XO replied, 'Do I know I'm hit?!' Then, softer, 'Yeah, how bad is it?' The wingman flew under the XO to inspect the damage;

'There were multiple holes in the wings and fuselage, with hydraulic fluid and fuel still leaking. He obviously only had fuselage fuel left, and the wing tanks had many holes. I told Quaid and he confirmed he had about 1100 lbs of fuel remaining. He said the controls felt stiff and sluggish, and he might have to disconnect the boost package (the same procedure that Al Crebo was also following at that very moment).'

The XO was still in command of the flight, however, and he tried to reassemble his aircraft. 'Eagle Three' and 'Eagle Four' were still in formation as the four aircraft joined on Al Crebo in 'Eagle Six', with 'Eagle Five' as his wingman. Gray continued;

'Crebo's A-4 was a sight to behold. He had no rudder, and fully half of the vertical stabiliser was gone. Holes the size of footballs and basketballs allowed the others to see right through the tail pipe in several places. Someone pointed out that viewed from dead astern, the horizontal stabilizer was twisted about three degrees out of alignment with the trailing edge of the wing. Every access panel in the fuselage had popped open from the force of the concussion.'

After Crebo ejected, the rest of the flight set up for their recovery aboard the 'Bonnie Dick'. Cdr Quaid called the ball, telling the LSO, 'I'm the guy with nothing!' He had lost most of his systems, and had to get aboard on his first pass, which he did. After cannibalising the A-4 for parts, the squadron pushed it over the side.

Intelligence reports revealed the North Vietnamese had fired more than 30 SA-2s at *Bon Homme Richard's* strike group. As now-retired airline captain Gray observed, 'This was just a prelude of things to come in the summer of 1967'.

INTENSE ACTION CONTINUES

Al Crebo's carrier had a lot going on as April turned to May. 'Bonnie Dick' was another 27-Charlie *Essex* conversion. The ship's name carried on the tradition of one of America's first men of war. John Paul Jones, the Scottish-born icon of the Revolution navy, had named his French-built ship after Ben Franklin's highly successful almanac. It was from the bloody deck of his sinking vessel that Jones gave what became the quintessential American war cry, 'I have not yet begun to fight!' With a clarion call like that, it was essential that America's Navy always keep active the name of that famous old ship. While not as modern as the bigger carriers, CVA-31 would make six war cruises in only six years.

The squadrons of CVW-21 had an active May, beginning with a MiG kill by an A-4 pilot. Although it was small and nimble, and had a fairly

heavy defensive armament with its two 20 mm cannon, the A-4 was a bomber. And again, although they certainly trained in aerial manoeuvres, mainly for defensive measures should they be attacked by enemy fighters, 'Scooter' pilots were, after all, attack aviators, earth movers, breakers of dykes. And although the A-4 would enjoy a secondary career as a highly successful adversary type, even having a starring role in the blockbuster 1986 film *Top Gun*, it was still, after all, a bomber.

Yet, attack pilots are akin to their fighter pilot brethren – aggressive, determined, and opportunistic. Often, the two types swap communities, cross-pollinate, as it is sometimes described. One such pilot was high-time F-8 Crusader 'driver' Lt Cdr T R Swartz, who decided that the place to be in the growing conflict was an A-4's cockpit. He was eventually assigned to VA-76, which had made one previous combat deployment, aboard *Enterprise* in 1965.

The North Vietnamese had steadily built up their fighter force with contributions from the Soviet Union and communist China. Flying an assortment of MiGs, but mainly the MiG-17 and MiG-21 (which was always in short supply), the Vietnamese People's Air Force (VPAF) had occasionally given US flight crews more than a little trouble. Each victory over a communist fighter was celebrated at both squadron and command level, with the victorious pilot usually whisked away to Saigon to answer media questions. The Navy's F-4 and F-8 squadrons were the main 'distributors of MiG parts', but Swartz and his A-4C contributed their share on 1 May during a trip to the large VPAF base at Kep, near Hanoi.

'TR' launched in A-4C BuNo 148609 'NP 685', along with seven other VA-76 A-4s. VF-24 F-8s and A-4s from VA-212 made up the rest of the strike package of 22 jets. Two of the F-8s turned back because of mechanical problems, leaving the rest of the strikes to press on. As they

VA-76's Lt Cdr T R Swartz registered the only MiG kill by a US Skyhawk. His aircraft (A-4C BuNo 148609) is shown here with its single red flag/yellow star victory marking below the cockpit. BuNo 148609 was eventually written off in a flying accident on 23 June 1972 while serving with NAS Oceana-based utility squadron VC-2 (*Jay Hargrove via Warren Thompson*)

Of the three main threats – AAA, SAMs and MiGs – facing Skyhawk pilots over North Vietnam, MiGs were considered a distant third in concern and effectiveness. Nonetheless, they were not to be ignored, and had to be figured into the pre-strike planning equation. Although unsophisticated in comparison with most of its American adversaries, the small MiG-17 (and its Chinese-built equivalent, the Shenyang J-5) was agile and carried three powerful cannon. These camouflaged MiG-17F 'Fresco-Cs' – dubbed 'Snakes' by their pilots – are from the VPAF's 923rd Fighter Regiment at Kep. This was almost certainly the unit that Lt Cdr T R Swartz and Lt John Waples engaged on 1 May 1967 (*via Istvan Toperczer*)

approached Kep, two MiG-17s appeared – a pair of F-8s from VF-24 broke off to pursue the interceptors. Lt Cdr Swartz was the leader of the flak suppressor section, and was thus carrying Zuni pods, which each contained four of the big rockets that were proving so effective against ground targets.

As the bombers hit the airfield, ultimately destroying as many as 30 MiGs on the ground, Swartz and his wingman, Lt John Waples, headed for flak sites on Kep's eastern side. Diving towards his target, Swartz saw two MiG-17s taxiing onto the runway preparing to take off. He and Waples fired their Zunis and destroyed the two enemy fighters.

As Swartz and Waples pulled up from their dive, they came under attack themselves as tracers flew by their canopies. Rolling their Skyhawks, they spotted two more MiGs that had sneaked up behind them. Waples called a warning and Swartz snap-rolled into a left turn. The MiGs tried to match the hard turn until Swartz pulled his control stick into his stomach. As the A-4 nearly stood on its tail, the VPAF pilots decided to return to their airfield. Waples fired his cannon at the departing enemy fighters, and it looked like he was hitting one of the MiGs when he ran out of bullets.

Swartz still had a few Zunis left, and he slid in behind the MiGs and fired one of his missiles, which failed to hit the target. He fired again, but could not wait to see if he had hit the MiG-17 in front of him because Waples called a third VPAF fighter sliding in on Swartz's tail. The Navy pilot racked his A-4 around to disrupt the MiG's set-up. Waples, however, watched as one of the first MiGs descended behind a hill. A few seconds later he saw a large column of black smoke.

By now Swartz had cleared his tail and gone after the second MiG, firing his cannon, but he too ran out of ammunition. Never intended as a primary air-to-air weapon, the A-4's twin cannon had a limited amount of ammunition, which had been recently further reduced to make space for additional electronic defence gear. T R Swartz received a Silver Star for his success, which was the only air-to-air kill made by an American A-4.

MORE LOSSES

Skyhawk squadrons from the other carriers were deeply involved in the bombing campaign that had come to symbolise the entire air war. *Enterprise* and *Hancock* sent their air groups over Haiphong, and, predictably, many A-4s were lost.

VA-113's Lt(jg) James S Graham was killed on 4 May during a mission near Thanh Hoa. It was his 173rd mission over Vietnam. One of four A-4Cs, his aircraft (BuNo 148514) was hit by flak as he dived on a SAM site. He ejected near a village and was seen to wave in his parachute, but he did not return with other PoWs in 1973. The Vietnamese returned his remains in 1985.

VA-93 lost Lt(jg) Robert E Wideman two days later during an armed reconnaissance mission south of Thanh Hoa. As he attacked river barges, AAA struck his A-4E (BuNo 151082) and he ejected to become a PoW.

On 10 May VA-94 lost A-4C BuNo 149509 and CVW-5 lost its leader, Cdr Roger M Netherland. The CAG had launched from *Hancock* with a section of flak suppressors. Approaching the airfield at Kien, near Haiphong, Cdr Netherland evaded two SAMs but not the third, which exploded under his aircraft. Although the stricken A-4 turned back towards the water, it was streaming fire and fuel. CAG might have been hurt, and therefore unable to prevent his A-4 from rolling inverted and hitting the water.

Yet another senior A-4 pilot was shot down on 18 May. Cdr Ken Cameron, XO of VA-76, led a strike against a shipping facility just north of Vinh. His A-4C (BuNo 147816) took a flak hit during the delivery dive and Cameron punched out. Although known to have been captured, news filtered out that he was in poor health, and Cameron sadly died in 1970 while in a PoW hospital. The North Vietnamese returned his remains in 1974 in what was one of the earliest repatriations.

A new weapon had entered the inventory in March. The AGM-62 Walleye was a television-guided glide bomb that the pilot could lock onto his target before launch. After being dropped, it continued homing in on the target while the pilot concentrated on evasive manoeuvres and getting away from enemy defences. VA-212 CO Cdr Homer L Smith made the first Walleye attack, going against military barracks at Sam Son on 11 March. He watched the weapon fly right through a window and explode inside the building. The next day saw three more Walleyes sent against the infamous Thanh Hoa Bridge. Although all three bombs hit the structure, they did not have enough explosive power to bring it down.

Cdr Smith was another A-4 leader who was captured and who died in captivity. On 20 May, he led an Alpha strike of 17 aircraft from CVW-21 against the thermal powerplant at Bac Giang, some 25 miles east of Hanoi. Smith sent a Walleye towards the plant and was pulling up when his A-4E (BuNo 149652) was hit by flak. The CO ejected and was captured. He was taken to the Hanoi Hilton, where he was soon undergoing excruciating torture. He apparently died while resisting such barbaric treatment.

Smith had received the Silver Star for an earlier mission in 1966. Now, he received a posthumous Navy Cross for his role in the Bac Giang strike, as well as the mission the previous day (19 May) against another thermal powerplant in Hanoi. He was also posthumously promoted to captain.

Flying the A-4 was obviously one of the most hazardous professions in 1967. The first half of the year was only part of the story.

VA-212 CO Cdr Homer Smith (right) stands with Lt Tom Taylor on the 'Bonnie Dick's' flightdeck before the first Walleye mission on 11 March 1967. Taylor had joined CVW-21 on temporary assignment from the Navy's weapons development centre at China Lake, in California, where he had worked extensively on developing delivery profiles for the AGM-62. Behind them is A-4E BuNo 149971, which survived several combat tours of Vietnam. In late 1973 it was one of 46 E-models quietly transferred to the Israeli Defence Force/Air Force as attrition replacements for A-4s lost during the Yom Kippur War, which had taken place in October of that year

A LONG YEAR

As we have seen, during the first six months of 1967 the war intensified to the extent that US aircraft and their crews were being lost on nearly every bombing raid that ventured into the hornets' nests around Hanoi and Haiphong. Cdr Bryan Compton, a native of Alabama and CO of VA-163 at this time, observed that negotiating the enemy's defences would be 'like walking through a cow pasture on a hot summer's afternoon'.

The A-4 units took the brunt of the losses. Certainly, the F-4 and A-6 squadrons suffered their share, and the Phantom IIs had to deal with the enemy's growing fighter strength. Truth be told, only one A-4 was confirmed lost to MiGs during the entire war – A-4C BuNo 147799 from VA-76, flown by Lt Cdr Charles D Stackhouse, as noted in the preceding chapter. After dropping his bombs on a POL mission near Haiphong, Stackhouse was attacked by MiG-17s that quickly shot him down. He ejected and spent the rest of the war as a PoW. In comparison, eight Navy F-4s and two A-6s were lost to VPAF MiGs.

The A-4's main nemesis was the concentrations of flak and SAM sites that ringed the capital and port, as well as around Vinh to the south.

Still paired with the 'Saints' of VA-163 aboard *Oriskany*, VA-164 began its third combat deployment in June 1967. It would be another hectic cruise, with the squadron losing 11 A-4s – four in four days. Three of the four pilots were recovered, but the fourth, Lt Cdr Richard D Hartman was captured and later died in prison. Hartman was the subject of a two-day SAR effort that claimed another A-4 from VA-164 and the four-man crew of an HS-2 SH-3A that tried to find the downed aviator.

The North Vietnamese seemed to have been replenished with ammunition and missiles, much to the dismay of CVW-16 aircrew. As retired Capt Bob Arnold wrote in the Winter 1990 issue of *The Hook*, 'There wasn't an easy target anywhere in the North'.

Lt Cdr Dean Cramer flew with VA-163. A former enlisted aviation electrician, his irrepressible outlook went with his call sign of 'Dynamite'. As the squadrons continued losing men, he directed the parachute riggers to change how the names were applied to the ready room chairs. Seating order was according to seniority. Normally, the chairs used head covers on which the individual pilot's name was embroidered. As someone was lost, the covers changed. Cramer

The *Essex*-class carriers featured a middle-deck elevator, as shown in this photo of *Hancock* crewmen moving VA-93 A-4E BuNo 151105 in early May 1967. Concern for how battle damage to the centrally located lift would affect the vessel's operational capability resulted in elevators being moved to the deck edge starting with *Midway* class carriers. This has subsequently been a design trait of all US 'flattops'. Both BuNo 151105 and BuNo 151049, attached to bow catapult one, would be lost in action over North Vietnam. 'NF 301' was downed by a SAM during an *Iron Hand* mission in support of a strike on the Do Xa transshipment point, 15 miles south of Hanoi, on 30 May 1967. The jet's pilot, VA-93 XO Cdr James Mehl, was forced to eject near Hung Yen and was immediately captured. 'NF 313' was transferred to VMA-121 upon the completion of VA-93's combat deployment, and the aircraft was shot down by small arms fire near Ba Long when strafing entrenched North Vietnamese Army troops on 5 May 1968. Its pilot, 1Lt T M Aiton, ejected and was rescued by a Marine Corps helicopter

told his enlisted members to use Velcro patches so that name tags could be removed as required. The riggers shook their heads but complied.

Bob Arnold recalled one particularly tough mission in July against a barracks compound just south of central Hanoi. Hoping to surprise the enemy, Arnold took his strikers directly towards downtown Hanoi. Perhaps the gunners on the ground would hold their fire, rather than risk shooting up their capital city. No such luck. The gunners were waiting.

'The strike group was hosed down all the way into the target area', Arnold remembered. Missiles and flak filled the skies, which were becoming increasingly overcast, making it hard for the pilots to see their targets. Deciding to abort the strike, the crews turned for home, but not before an F-8 was brought down by a SAM.

A few days later, Arnold was leading another package to the same target. There had been a major change in the A-4s' load-out. Normally, the jet flew with two external fuel tanks, extending the range. Of course, that extra fuel came at a price in reduced bomb load. To make sure they did some real damage to the enemy barracks, the eight A-4Es dispensed with their fuel tanks and were now carrying ten Mk 82 500-lb bombs – a fairly good load for the Skyhawk. Eighty 500-lb bombs could, indeed, do major damage. There was also the rationale that the normal number of 14 A-4s to carry 80 bombs was reduced by nearly half, thereby putting less jets and pilots in harm's way. It looked like a good decision all around.

After planning well into the night, crews turned in to get a few hours' sleep. When they awoke and made their way to the briefing room, a nasty surprise waited for them. The intel folks had been busy putting different coloured pushpins all over the planning chart, indicating the greatly increased number of flak and SAM sites now known to be in the area that would receive the Alpha strike's attention. The pilots gasped in disbelief.

The strike force launched and found the waiting A-3 tankers. With their extra bombs, the A-4s needed to top off as soon as possible before heading north. Refuelling took longer than anticipated, and the mission was soon 40 minutes behind schedule. Coasting in, Arnold checked his force – eight bombers, four *Iron Hand* A-4s with their four F-8 escorts, and four F-8 fighter escorts. The 20-jet package headed inland.

The approach to the target was quiet. No missiles or flak came up to greet the Navy aircraft as their pilots searched for their targets. But the enemy was not asleep because the earphones in their helmets told each pilot the ground radars were tracking them. Suddenly, 85 mm flak – amongst the heaviest in the North Vietnamese inventory – appeared. Then the missiles came up. Calls to break or dive peppered the airwaves. Estimates of 30 to 44 missiles were given later.

The defensive barrage forced the strike force down to a lower altitude, where they dropped their bombs and turned for the water. Arnold found himself alone with his wingman at 3500 ft making 400 knots. The two pilots still had their ordnance. The wingman attacked first but missed, and Arnold went next. As he dived on the target, he could see occasional flak bursts. The barracks filled his windscreen as he dropped his load.

Seconds seemed liked hours as Arnold felt each bomb drop. Relieved of its load, the A-4 gathered speed as the pilot stood the jet on a wing and made for the safety of the water. He chanced a look back to see his bombs hit directly on target – an attack pilot's dream.

Cdr Peter W Sherman, CO of VA-56, was killed in action on 10 June 1967 while leading an *Iron Hand* section. He had been in command of the unit for just three months

Going as fast as he could, Arnold took his section out of danger, followed by a single SAM that tracked him for a while, but he evaded it. After landing back aboard, he found that initial assessments gave destruction as 50 percent, which seemed to satisfy the higher-ups, given the level of difficulty for a target so close to Hanoi. Fortunately, although one A-4 was badly shot up, everyone had come back.

A LONG SUMMER

Along with the rest of the TF 77 squadrons on duty in the South China Sea, Skyhawk units continued flying the most hazardous missions up north. By August, the usual workups on *Dixie Station* were forgotten as the requirements were decidedly farther north.

VA-76 lost two A-4Cs on 14 July, including one flown by the CO, Cdr (later RAdm) Robert B Fuller. Leading a strike against a railway bridge, Fuller, in BuNo147709, took a SAM hit just as he began his delivery. The CO kept going and dropped his bombs, even though his jet was now streaming a trail of fire and fuel. Ejecting as it began to roll, Fuller was the second VA-76 skipper to be lost in eight months – he had taken over after Cdr A D McFall had been killed in an operational mishap in December 1966. Fuller was captured and spent the rest of the war as a PoW.

The second VA-76 pilot downed on the 14th was Lt J N Donis, who ejected from A-4C BuNo 147759 after it was hit by flak during an armed reconnaissance mission. He was soon rescued by a Navy helicopter.

Skyhawks from *Intrepid* and 'Bonnie Dick' were also lost during this time. One of CVS-11's VSF-3 aviators, Lt(jg) Fred Kasch was killed during an attack on the railway yard at Hai Duong on 2 July. His A-4B (BuNo 145002) was one of the few 'Bravos' to see combat. Struck by flak while pulling out of his dive, Kasch and his wingman headed for the coast. The jet had been hit in the engine, which steadily lost power, causing the A-4 to lose altitude as the pilot struggled to make the water. At barely 500 ft, Kasch's wingman called for him to eject, then lost sight of him. As he swung around to check for Kasch's parachute, the wingman saw the crash site in a village. The Vietnamese returned Kasch's remains in 1988.

A second VSF-3 aviator was lost on 3 October when Lt(jg) A D Perkins was downed in A-4B BuNo 142114. Fortunately, Perkins was retrieved from Haiphong Harbour by an H-2.

Along with A-4s from VA-15 and VA-34, VSF-3 Skyhawks engaged at least six VPAF MiG-17s on 5 October 1967 during an Alpha strike near the fighter airfield at Kien An, south-east of Hanoi. Luck was against the American aviators in one way or another, however, as jammed cannon, expended ordnance, faulty radios and low fuel conspired to prevent anything but

An ordnanceman loads 20 mm shells into an A-4C from VA-36 aboard *Intrepid* during CVW-10's bloody 1967 combat cruise. The three Skyhawk units embarked in the vessel lost no fewer than 11 aircraft in combat during 103 days on the line, with a 12th jet being lost during operational flying. Three pilots were killed, three captured and six recovered. The A-4C could carry 200 rounds for its twin Colt Mk 12 20 mm cannon. Although a handy weapon for strafing when serviceable, the Mk 12 was prone to jamming

possible hits on the fast-turning MiGs, which soon departed the area. The disappointed A-4 pilots headed back to *Intrepid*.

During this period, VA-212 suffered several losses, too, as did VA-163 and VA-146. It was a dark time that was about to get even darker.

THE *FORRESTAL* FIRE

The four *Forrestals* (*Forrestal*, *Saratoga*, *Ranger* and *Independence*) would all make combat deployments to Vietnam, with *Ranger* having made two by 1967. Normally assigned to the Atlantic Fleet, USS *Forrestal* (CVA-59) was sent to the Pacific to help with the war in South-east Asia. Leaving its home port of Norfolk, Virginia, on 6 June 1967, the vessel had CVW-17 embarked, which included A-4E squadrons VA-46 and VA-106. Arriving on *Yankee Station* on 25 July, CVW-17 had generated 150 sorties over the next four days without loss.

Just before 1100 hrs on 29 July, a second strike was preparing to launch when a Zuni rocket was accidentally fired from an F-4, hitting an A-4. The ensuing conflagration was among the worst in Navy history. Just which 'Scooter' was hit has never been determined. Many reports give the aircraft (BuNo 149996, 'AA 416') of Lt Cdr John S McCain, and movie clips from cameras that monitor deck action showed McCain, scion of one of America's most well-known Navy families, hurriedly evacuating his burning jet, rolling over the cockpit sill and jumping to the deck. However, the Navy's JAGMAN report indicates that the Zuni hit BuNo 150064 'AA 405', killing pilot Lt Cdr Fred White.

The fire caused on-deck ordnance to explode, adding to the flames that engulfed the entire aft end of the deck. Nearby ships hurried to help the stricken carrier. The memory of the previous year's shipboard fire on *Oriskany* was fresh in everyone's mind. That carrier, now repaired and back in the fight, stood by to help with fire fighting and medical aid.

Although the fire on the flightdeck was under control in an hour, secondary fires below decks took 12 hours to subdue. When it was over, the toll was 134 fatalities and 21 jets (including 11 A-4Es), with 43 other aeroplanes damaged. The cost to repair CVA-59 was estimated at $72 million. *Forrestal* arrived back in Norfolk on 14 September to begin the repair process. It never deployed to South-east Asia again. As a result of the *Forrestal* fire, rockets were eventually banned from shipboard use.

On 19 July, *Constellation's* CVW-14 had attacked an unusual target – a SAM site inside a soccer stadium between Hanoi and Haiphong. An RA-5C of RVAH-12 had brought back photographs showing the site, and several attacks were launched. VA-146's CO, Cdr (later VAdm) Robert F Dunn, led the first attack, damaging three SA-2s and their launchers. Dunn would receive the Silver Star later in the cruise.

Predictably, the North Vietnamese cried foul about the attack on the stadium missile site, calling it 'an act of pure air piracy'. One of the enemy's catch phrases during the war when referring to American flight

VA-106's CAG jet prepares to launch from USS *Forrestal* during the first hectic sorties of CVA-59's aborted cruise. 'AJ 300' carries Zuni rocket pods identical to those that caused the disastrous fire on 29 July 1967

Cdr Robert Dunn briefs his VA-146 pilots for a mission from 'Connie' during the unit's war cruise in 1967. Dunn received two Silver Stars for his exploits over Vietnam, and eventually commanded the carrier USS *Saratoga* (CV-60). Achieving flag rank, he was Commander Naval Air Forces Atlantic during operations against Libya in 1986. As Deputy Chief of Naval Operations (Air), at age 58, he made one more carrier landing in a *single*-seat F/A-18 just before retiring

VA-146 A-4C BuNo 147841 carries an AGM-12C Bullpup missile on its No 1 stores station. The big Bullpup was not as successful as the Walleye. To launch it, the pilot had to set up a low-powered glide at 20,000 ft, with a release at 18,000 ft. Using a small control stick in the cockpit, the pilot then had to fly the missile down to impact, which normally occurred when the A-4 had itself descended down to about 12,000 ft – right in the heart of the enemy's defence envelope. As VAdm Dunn observed, 'the enemy would begin tossing lead at you from the moment they saw you start a glide and spotted the Bullpup detach'. This rather lop-sided underwing stores configuration would not have been as much trouble as might first appear following the missile's launch. Adm Dunn continues, 'the pilot would burn fuel out of the drop tank right after take-off, and it would either be empty or nearly so at the time of missile launch. It was definitely not a preferred configuration, but it could be handled, especially by a "World Famous Blue Diamond" pilot!' When you're the CO, pride in your squadron comes first and foremost, even 40 years after the event! This aircraft was one of 70 surplus C-model jets bought from US surplus stocks by the Republic of Singapore Air Force in 1980 and rebuilt as an A-4S

crews was 'Yankee air pirates'. The aviators loved it, and quickly referred to themselves as such, sporting patches with the moniker. Still, the media picked up on these reports, feeding the anti-war sentiments plaguing the US, as well as other countries sympathetic to the communist cause.

Cdr Dunn and his unit attacked an airfield on 1 October. As he rolled into his dive, he saw an aircraft taxiing toward the runway. Of all things it appeared to be a World War 2 era piston-engined fighter (possibly a Yak-11). Communist countries that were clients of the USSR and China used such aircraft as trainers. Nevertheless, Dunn wanted to destroy it;

'I was in my dive, and too late to adjust my aim point enough to hit the aircraft, so after release I climbed and rolled back in on a second pass. An ironclad rule was to make only one pass, and no more. It was proven early in the war that more than one pass will probably get you shot down. But I had reason to violate the rule, and I did. I came around, charged my guns with 40 rounds, and then the God damn guns jammed!'

Dunn had been the squadron XO in 1966 during the *Ranger* cruise. Originally slated to go to VA-113, his orders were changed when 'Blue Diamonds' skipper Cdr Hugh Loheed was shot down and killed on 1 February 1966. His XO, Cdr Al Schaufelberger, 'fleeted up' to the command position, and Dunn was sent to be his 'exec', the two men duly forming a bond that carried the squadron through some rough times.

For his oral history recorded by the US Naval Institute, retired VAdm Dunn remembered the 'Charlie' model Skyhawk;

'VA-146's A-4Cs had three weapons stations – one on the centreline and one inboard under each wing. On each of the wing racks we would usually mount a triple ejector rack (TER), and on the centreline a 300-gallon fuel tank. On each TER would be either three Mk 81 250-lb or two Mk 82 500-lb bombs. Once in a while, we would carry rockets or, very occasionally, a Bullpup missile. For specific targets, we might carry two Mk 83 1000-lb bombs, one on each wing station, the TER having been removed. There were also times we would carry two 300-gallon fuel

tanks, one under each wing, with a multiple ejector rack (MER) on the centre station. The Bullpup could also be carried on the centre station.'

The intense response by the North Vietnamese to US strikes in the early summer of 1967 eventually resulted in the defenders running out of ammunition and missiles – at least for a time – in late July. Although the communists would turn on their tracking radars, alerting the incoming strikers that they had been spotted, the usual flak and SAMs failed to materialise, leaving the relieved Americans to exit the target areas after dropping their bombs. But the respite lasted for only a few days, and by early August the AAA and SAMs were back in spades.

On 21 August, 80 SAMs were launched at attackers from *Constellation*, *Intrepid* and *Oriskany*. Everything from supply depots to railway yards and airfields was hit with bombs, rockets and Walleyes. Even PT boat bases near Haiphong came under attack by A-4s from *Oriskany*, which sunk three of the small craft. Although no Skyhawks were lost during this day of heavy action, 'Connie's' air wing lost three A-6As from VA-196.

Cdr Bryan Compton, the CO of VA-163, led his A-4s against the Hanoi thermal powerplant, which had received so much attention the previous May. Predictably, the Vietnamese had repaired the damaged plant and placed several new flak sites around it. Compton's force fired five Walleyes, three hitting a generator and two hitting a boiler, producing columns of heavy black and white smoke that rose high over the entire complex. He later recalled;

'This was the first fixed target that we were scheduled to strike that was worth more than the cost of the ordnance we put into it. We were thus excited when we got a chance to devise a plan to take it out.

'During a turn-around at Lemoore in early 1967, VA-163's A-4Es were outfitted to use the Walleye, which was a new self-guiding glide bomb. We trained on the beach with it and had used it in combat on some lightly defended targets like railway bridges and tunnels. The Walleye locked onto visual contacts and was a very accurate weapon with considerable punch. Particularly important was the fact that you didn't have to remain in a dive or even in visual contact with the target after missile launch. It took little work to get trained to use it.

'After we returned to the line on the 1967 cruise, the tempo had picked up, with very little in North Vietnam now off limits. Although the number of Walleyes was limited, most of the squadron's experienced pilots had a chance to use one on either a bridge or similar target.

'When we got tasked to hit the powerplant in August, a major concern was to have as simultaneous an impact with six Walleyes as possible. To do this, we had to fan out the six A-4s carrying the missiles 15-20 miles from the target so that we all approached from different headings.

'After working up this Rube Goldberg attack plan with Lt Cdr Jerry Breast, Lt Cdr Cramer, Lt Cdr Busey and others, I had to brief the "heavies" starting with Adm Curtis, CARDIV 9, aboard *Oriskany*, then CTF 77 and finally VAdm John Bringle, Commander Seventh Fleet, aboard *Oklahoma City*. After the briefings, the strike was on standby.'

The previous day, 20 August, Compton had been on a road reconnaissance, and as a result almost missed the big mission;

'We had bombed a truck when I got tagged with a 37 mm shell in the right aileron. My wingman and I diverted to the Marine Corps base at

Looking every inch the tough, capable squadron leader that he was, VA-163 CO Cdr Bryan Compton squints into the camera. He eventually retired from the Navy with the rank of rear admiral (*via Bryan Compton*)

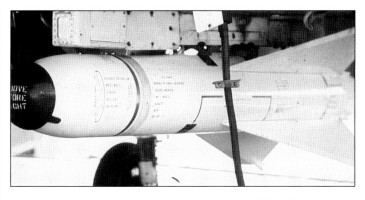

This close-up of a live AGM-62 Walleye glide bomb shows the weapon's cruciform tail-wing design (*via Bryan Compton*)

Taken on the momentous mission of 21 August 1967, this photograph shows two VA-163 A-4Es, each armed with a single Walleye. Squadron commander Compton is flying 'AH 307'. His position indicates that this photo was taken early in the mission right after launch, as the formation has yet to organise itself with him in the lead (*via Bryan Compton*)

Chu Lai. Thinking the strike on the powerplant was imminent, I sweet-talked a sergeant into swapping an aileron and we were out of there with bombs and a new aileron!

'After a short visit to the beach, we went back to *Oriskany*, where the go-ahead for the powerplant strike had been received. We scheduled myself, Lt Cdrs Jim Busey, Jerry Breast and John Miles, Lt Vance Shufeldt and Lt(jg) Fritz Schroeder, with Lt Cdr Dean Cramer and Lt(jg) Dave Carey as the spares. We cleaned up our jets – no tanks or weapons, except the Walleyes. We dispensed with TARCAP, but had them standing by off the beach, along with the tanker. We also dispensed with both the *Iron Hand* SAM suppressors and the flak suppressors. And because we weren't going to carry external fuel tanks, I asked the ship's navigator to get us up north, close to the PIRAZ station, which he did. PIRAZ stood for Positive Identification Radar Advisory Zone, and was the name for the ships that provided information on everything from navigation to airborne threats.

'The flight was scheduled for the following day, 21 August. Lt Cdr Miles had an airborne abort and thus Lt Cdr Cramer launched as the spare. He had taken Lt(jg) Carey's jet when he (Cramer) couldn't get his Walleye to check out before launching – RHIP (rank has its privileges!).'

Some 20 SAMs were fired amid a barrage of heavy AAA. Although no aeroplanes were lost, several sustained heavy damage, including those flown by Lt Cdr (later Adm) James B Busey IV and Lt Cdr Dean E Cramer. Busey's A-4 landed with 127 holes in the starboard wing alone. Its starboard horizontal stabiliser was gone, as was the starboard elevator. The groundcrew also counted 85 to 110 holes in Cramer's jet.

Dean Cramer remembered his part in the mission for Jeffrey L Levinson's account of carrier aviation in Vietnam, *Alpha Strike Vietnam*;

'I was hit in my dive, my glide, by an 85 mm shell that exploded beneath my jet and blew it inverted. I got back level, but the Walleye screen was all screwed up, and I could hear the bomb, with a thin, tin-like skin, tearing away from the plane. The shell – and I didn't know this – had punched a small hole in one wing, which was bleeding fuel and leaving a white vapour trail behind me. Every God damn SAM and flak site in Hanoi, I'm convinced, was shooting at me.'

Finally, a 37 mm shell struck Cramer's jet, which began to burn.

'Okay, I'm hit', he called on what he thought was a dedicated tactical frequency. 'I'm on fire and coming out'. Cramer's private little hell was being broadcast throughout his carrier. As he called for help, heading his burning Skyhawk back for the water, an F-8 joined on him hoping to escort him back to the ship. Now more than anything else, he needed fuel. An A-4 tanker could only give him a few gallons because it had problems with its buddy store, and a second 'Scooter' could not reel out its hose. Finally, an A-3 appeared, but could only give 200 lbs because Cramer's A-4 was so badly damaged. But it was enough – just barely.

'The hole in the port wing was the attention getter', Cramer recalled. 'It was a direct hit from a 37 mm shell, and it burned from Hanoi until I reached the coast. I could see the fire in the wing and I knew I had other damage. But other than all of my engine and fuel gauges being out, I didn't have the foggiest. It still flew, so I took it home'.

Cleared for a straight-in approach, he dived for the deck, only to find that Busey had also been cleared in on another frequency. Breaking off for his squadronmate, Cramer came around for another try when Busey boltered. Once both men were safely down, they were only too glad to take some 'medicinal' brandy.

'I advised the ship that the wing might fall off on landing', Cramer said, 'so they should be prepared. I did not expect it to burn on deck as I could not have had much fuel left. The wing was empty and the fuselage tank must have been damn close'.

Cdr Compton and Lt Cdr Busey both received the Navy Cross for the mission – one of the few times that pilots from the same squadron received this high honour for the same mission. Lt Cdr Cramer received the DFC, and he would eventually accumulate five such medals during the course of nearly 400 combat missions from three different carriers.

Commenting on the A-4, and having *Oriskany's* crew listening in on the mission, Compton recalled, 'It was a tribute to the sturdiness of the A-4 that Cramer managed to bring it back. After he landed, we were all overwhelmed by the tremendous reception that we got from our crew. We had been performing for a large audience'.

Five weeks prior to this mission, VA-163 pilot Lt Cdr Marvin D Reynolds had been awarded the Navy Cross for his part in a SAR mission on 17 July. Lt Cdr Butch Verich from VF-162 – one of two Crusader fighter squadrons aboard *Oriskany* – had been shot down on 16 July (for the second time in a year) and was on the ground waiting for rescue only 16 miles from Hanoi. As the light was failing, he had to spend the night where he was, but at first light on the 17th, an SH-3 from *Hornet* began making its way back over the beach towards the stranded aviator.

Verich's position was close to an enemy flak site, which began firing on the helicopter. Lt Cdr Reynolds, leading a section of A-4Es from VA-163, headed for the action, establishing contact with the helicopter comman-der before pick-up could be made. Low on fuel, Reynolds took his section to a waiting tanker and then rejoined the H-3, which by now had verified Verich's identity. Avoiding three SAMs and flak, Reynolds and his wing-man attacked the nearby flak site and put it out of action. The helicopter crew was now able to retrieve the F-8 pilot. On the egress route, Reynolds' section attacked and silenced another dangerous flak site.

Lt Neil R Sparks Jr, the pilot in command of the SH-3, also received the Navy Cross for his vital role in this rescue.

Cdr Compton had also been supporting the rescue mission, and in doing so almost got himself a MiG. As attention was naturally focused on

VA-163's energetic air warrior Lt Cdr Dean Cramer, better known as 'Dynamite', grins by his A-4

the helicopter's exit after picking up Lt Cdr Verich, a North Vietnamese MiG-21 pilot decided to sneak in behind the lumbering SH-3. Compton was flying solo because his wingman had to abort. His A-4 had been armed as a flak suppressor and was carrying a load of Zunis and cluster bomb units – not exactly the best load-out for shooting down MiGs. He still had his two 20 mm cannon, however, although with a limited supply of ammunition. Compton recalled;

'Trailing the helicopter as it withdrew, with the A-1 escort and F-8 fighter cover, who were at about 4000 ft, I spotted a MiG-21 coming down from the north, closing on the Crusaders' "six o'clock". I was about 5000 ft above the F-8s. As he was pretty close to a firing position, I fired my Zunis to force him to break off, but I was too far out to do much. Moments later I was in a perfect position for a rendezvous, and ended up less than 100 ft from the MiG's "six o'clock".'

Compton fired one round of 20 mm ammunition but then his guns jammed! However, by this time the MiG had broken off its attack and turned for home.

'I was doing my best to keep up and call in the "Superheats", which was the call sign for VF-162. I thought we had a real hamburger (the MiG pilot), but he kicked it into 'burner and was soon gone.'

Frustrated at not getting any response to catch what seemed to be 'meat on the table', Compton flew back to the carrier, where everyone agreed it had been a lost opportunity.

August 1967 proved to be one of the most dangerous months of the war, with pilots reporting 249 SAM launches. Sixteen Navy aircraft had been lost to enemy defences.

THE BRIDGE CAMPAIGN

Much of the communist supply trail immediately south of the main complex of Hanoi and Haiphong was made up of railway and highway bridges that spanned various rivers. Naturally, a large portion of the *Rolling Thunder* activity focused on destroying these vital conduits. A lot of ordnance was expended and many men and their aircraft were lost attacking the structures, which were usually well defended. One

Despite being grievously wounded over North Vietnam on 20 November 1967, Lt(jg) Dennis R Earl of VA-163 brought his A-4E (BuNo 152003) back to *Oriskany* and successfully took the barrier

Lt(jg) Earl is carefully lifted from his cockpit. He had been wounded by a 14.7 mm machine gun round that came through the cockpit, struck his left foot and continued into his right leg. Following six hours of surgery, Earl made a full recovery. BuNo 152003 was lost in an operational accident in the Gulf of Tonkin on 13 August 1969. It was serving with VA-144 aboard CVA-31 at the time

frustrating aspect of these targets was that even though a bridge might be destroyed or badly damaged, the North Vietnamese often performed miraculous feats of engineering by hastily repairing or rebuilding them. Another major attack was then required, with subsequent losses.

The USAF focused its attention on the Paul Doumer Bridge over the Red River near Hanoi. Even though the bridge was heavily damaged in August 1967, it was back in operation within two months. One bridge, however, became a legend – the Thanh Hoa Railway Bridge over the Ma River, 80 miles south of Hanoi. It eventually symbolised the heartbreaking frustration of US aircrews, for in three-and-a-half years, from March 1965 to November 1968, when another of the Johnson bombing halts was instituted, nearly 700 sorties were flown against the bridge. As noted on page 44, even three Walleye glide bombs hitting the heavy structure in March 1967 failed to bring it completely down.

VAdm Dunn remembered his impressions of the Thanh Hoa Railway Bridge, and the overall bridge-busting campaign;

'It was a big trestle bridge that stood out from everything else so well that we felt we just had to get it. After a while it became a symbol, to both the Vietnamese and us. The approaches to the bridge looked like the craters of the moon, and there was an inordinate amount of AAA in the vicinity. We didn't drop it, and neither did anyone else, until 1972.'

The final three months of 1967 were as eventful as the preceding quarter. *Coral Sea* arrived on *Yankee Station* in late August and quickly got back into the combat routine. Its embarked air wing, CVW-15, had brought a mix of aircraft, including F-4s, A-1s (VA-25 was making the last combat deployment for the single-seat veteran) and A-4E units VA-153 and VA-155. The 'Blue Tail Flies' of VA-153 lost their first A-4 on 29 August when Lt Michael J Allard apparently stalled his jet (BuNo 151025) while delivering old, unwieldy Mk 117 750-lb bombs.

Lt(jg) Fred Fortner of sister squadron VA-155 was killed on 17 October apparently from a malfunction with the 2.75-in rockets he had just fired at a storage site. Although he was able to head towards the water, he called that his controls were frozen. No one saw him eject and his A-4 (BuNo 152038) crashed.

A truly unfortunate loss occurred on 25 November. VA-155's popular CO, Cdr William H Searfus, had been in the ready room preparing for a mission. Answering a request from his maintenance department for a pilot to man an A-4 for a power check – something usually delegated to a junior aviator – Searfus responded that he would accommodate the maintainers on the deck. Thus, strapped in, he was taxiing A-4E BuNo 150037 when the powerful jet blast from a nearby F-4 blew the Skyhawk overboard, a drop of some 70 ft. The A-4 hit the water inverted and the CO drowned. Searfus had only taken command in June, and his death hit the air wing particularly hard.

However, the big losers in terms of A-4s continued to be *Oriskany* and *Intrepid*. The 'O Boat' was on its third war cruise, while 'The Fighting I' was on its second. *Oriskany* would lose eight A-4Es by the time it left the line in early November. *Intrepid's* three A-4 units would lose 12 jets.

Some ready room theories put forward to explain these losses considered that the A-4C's engine put out too much smoke, making it easier to track by the flak gunners. Then there were the weather prophets

Coral Sea is seen underway in the Gulf of Tonkin during its 1967-68 war cruise, when the vessel spent 132 days on the line. The veteran ship survived long enough to undertake a final combat deployment in 1986 to Libya, when its F/A-18 Hornets made the aircraft's combat debut. The commander of the carrier battle group was RAdm Jerry Breast, a 1967-68 veteran of VA-163 who had been hastily recalled from his position as head of the Naval Safety Center in Norfolk, Virginia (*PH1 R A Elder*)

who maintained that *Oriskany* always 'enjoyed' good weather for its deployments. Other carriers, like *Coral Sea*, seemed to be scheduled during the monsoon that enveloped the region in rain, low ceilings and reduced visibility from December to March. Bad weather made for cancelled missions and reduced loss rates. Of course, scuttlebutt and speculation were just that. The missions also launched in the worst conditions, and jets went down and their pilots died or were captured.

From late August to early November, VA-163 lost seven A-4s and VA-164 four. One of the 'Saints' pilots shot down was Lt Cdr John S McCain, survivor of the *Forrestal* fire in July. Anxious to continue his combat tour, he had cross-decked to *Oriskany's* air wing. On 26 October, flying A-4E BuNo 149959, McCain entered his dive toward a thermal powerplant near Hanoi. He was quickly targeted by a SAM battery and its missile took off most of his Skyhawk's right wing. There was little he could do to retain control and he ejected right into the heart of the city. Evasion was impossible, and thus McCain began five years of torture and barbarous incarceration. Indeed, it would be a long journey from a filthy prison cell at the Hanoi Hilton to the halls of Congress.

In one of his periodic newsletters to the squadron families back home, Cdr Compton wrote:

'2 November 1967

'The line period we have just concluded has been the heaviest to date. Except for a two-day period while we were evading Typhoon *Carla* and the last two days, the weather has been very good. As the north-east monsoon, which brings poor weather over North Vietnam, generally comes in October, the long spell of Indian summer weather was somewhat unexpected. We have exploited the good weather in major strike efforts. Many of these have been previously unstruck targets such as Phuc Yen and Kien An airfields and the Haiphong Barracks area south-east of the city.

'As somewhat of a change, we flew a good number of night sorties, either having two large strikes during the day followed by three night cycles, or starting about 0100 hrs with three night cycles followed by two large day strikes. As we launch all of the aircraft that can be made ready for a major strike, we ordinarily stand down for two hours between flights to rearm the aircraft and have them ready for the next go.'

On 2 November VA-164's Lt(jg) Fred Knapp (in A-4E BuNo 151895) was killed during an armed reconnaissance mission, possibly from flak hits during his delivery dive on a truck.

Eight days earlier, on 25 October, a wayward Zuni ignited a fire aboard *Coral Sea* – the recent ban of aerial rockets generated by the *Forrestal* blaze had yet to take effect. The rocket was being handled by ordnancemen on the mess deck – not unusual, as armament assembly spaces were normally adjacent to enlisted eating facilities. The warhead lodged in a bulkhead (wall) and had to be defused. Two other rockets had been activated before the fire was under control. Eight men had been burned to varying degrees, and the medical team worked long into the night to treat the injured sailors. Three eventually died. There were other peripheral problems caused by the heat and smoke that affected other crewmen.

Although not as big as the previous carrier fires, this one was bad enough. What made the event more tragic was that many of the families of the men aboard the vessel learned about it from reports in the press, instead of through the normal Navy casualty reporting network.

VA-155 lost Lt Cdr Wilmer P Cook on 22 December. Flying another armed reconnaissance mission in A-4E BuNo 152071, he had bombed one of the many pontoon bridges in North Vietnam and may have run into debris. His wingman reported seeing fire, then lost sight of his flight lead. He soon saw the crash site and called for a SAR helicopter, and although the crew of the latter saw Cook's body – still in his parachute not far from his A-4 – they could not land because of enemy ground fire. The North Vietnamese returned his remains in 1989.

VA-164 participated in what became the longest single MiG engagement of the war on 14 December. Four camouflaged MiG-17s tried to bounce an A-4 flown by Lt Chuck Nelson, who was on an *Iron Hand* mission. The escorting F-8s from VF-162 turned to meet the threat, and the ensuing dogfight took the MiGs and American fighters down almost to ground level.

Three MiGs broke off, but one stayed behind to fight, and to the grudging admiration of the Crusader drivers, he gave a good account of himself until Lt Dick Wyman brought him down with a Sidewinder. While he was busy trying to fly his Skyhawk, Lt Nelson also took a series of colour photographs of the green-and-brown MiG that quickly became some of the most popular air-to-air shots of the war.

A new jet joined operations in December 1967, and although the initial model was rather basic when viewed from the perspective of later variants to come, Vought's A-7A Corsair II was obviously the next generation. The trusty, tough little A-4 was on its way to retiring from combat operations. Many Skyhawk units began their final deployments then returned home to transition to the A-7, or decommission. But that all lay in the future. There was still a lot of war to be fought now, and there was room enough for both the Skyhawk and Corsair II.

Cdr William F Span, XO of VA-164, heads north in A-4E BuNo 151194 'AH 406' on 21 November 1967. His jet is armed with a Bullpup missile and iron bombs. After more than 20 years of service (which ended with Reserve-manned Marine Corps unit VMA-131, based at NAS Willow Grove, in Pennsylvania), this aircraft was retired in the late 1980s. Subsequently assigned to the National Museum of Naval Aviation, the jet is presently on loan to the Pacific Coast Air Museum in Santa Rosa, California (*via Robert Lawson*)

BATTLES AND BOMBING HALTS

With the heavy action of 1967 behind them, the carriers and their air wings took a break for Christmas, hoping the enemy would do the same. However, as with other bombing halts, the North Vietnamese used the break to move supplies south. Photo-reconnaissance flights showed what everyone knew was happening. President Johnson's carrot of a bombing halt was simply

not working. In the open and under the cover of darkness, trucks, bicycles, mules and human transporters flooded the Ho Chi Minh Trail – the main supply route that ran through Laos and into South Vietnam.

VA-164 A-4E BuNo 151133 became 1968's first Skyhawk casualty when its pilot, Lt George F Schindelar, was forced to eject due to the jet suffering control restrictions during an armed reconnaissance mission on New Year's Day. Fortunately, he was rescued. VA-112's A-4C BuNo 148486, flown by Lt Cdr Ed Estes, was downed by a SAM 48 hours later. Estes, on his 91st mission, was leading an *Iron Hand* flight near Haiphong when his cockpit filled with smoke and he ejected into captivity. VA-144 XO Cdr Robert J Schweitzer was next. On 5 January his A-4E (BuNo 152074) was hit by flak and he too ejected and was captured.

The final A-4 loss of the first week of 1968 was tragic. Lt(jg) Ralph Foulks of VA-163 had been shot down the previous October but had been rescued. However, on 5 January his luck ran out during a night armed reconnaissance mission. Diving on trucks, his leader lost contact with the pilot, and ultimately it was assumed that Foulks had fallen victim to flak seen in the target area. His remains were returned in 1988.

A-4E BuNo 151152 from VA-164 was lost on 11 January. Lt Cdr Denis R Weichman attacked a bridge in Laos and was hit by small arms fire as he pulled up from his run. With his engine vibrating and the temperature gauge rising, he headed for the water, some distance away. Finally over the South China Sea, but still several miles from *Oriskany*, Weichman ejected after the A-4 started to burn. Picked up by a helicopter, he later told his wife that it seemed 'forever' before he was rescued. Enemy boats were coming for him, but they were kept at bay by members of his flight, who dived and strafed the oncoming vessels. When she asked him if he was not afraid of sharks, he replied that he was more concerned about the venomous sea snakes that swam in those waters.

A-4C BuNo 147721 'NH 401' returns to *Kitty Hawk* after a mission in January 1968. VA-112 was one of the last Skyhawk units to operate from a 'big deck' during the war. This aircraft was sent to the Military Aircraft Storage and Disposition Center at Davis-Monthan AFB, Arizona, in August 1970 and was eventually scrapped

Cdr Charles Brown was VA-112's penultimate CO, leading the unit from November 1967 through to September 1968

Denis Weichman had received his wings in March 1957 and had flown Skyraiders with VA-25. After a shore tour as a flight instructor, he went to Vietnam in 1964 as an advisor to the VNAF. Standing nearly 6 ft 6 in, he towered over his pupils, but Weichman's easy smile and piloting skills quickly helped him establish himself. During this time, he began flying night combat missions in C-123 cargo aeroplanes, dropping and re-supplying saboteurs in North Vietnam. Thus, when he returned to the Navy and moved to the A-4, he had already seen some action. Weichman made two combat cruises with VA-164 in 1966-67. In fact, he had just launched from *Oriskany* when the disastrous fire broke out. 'My room was destroyed', he remembered. 'It was very demoralising and very sad'.

Weichman participated in strikes throughout the deployment, hitting the north-east sector of the Hanoi-Haiphong area, including the MiG base at Phuc Yen. He received the Silver Star for a mission on 24 October when he led eight jets tasked with missile suppression ahead of a major strike against Phuc Yen. Running in at low-level prior to conducting a successful loft delivery of one of his Shrike anti-radar missiles against an occupied SAM battery, his A-4E (BuNo 151194) sustained many hits from flak. Weichman also had to evade several SAM launches.

Minutes later, the determined aviator attacked a second SAM site, and this time he was opposed by heavy 85 mm flak. Missiles passed him from nearly every direction, their explosions occasionally sending shrapnel into his jet, knocking out his radio and navigational equipment. Finally, with his A-4 threatening to shake itself apart, Weichman headed back toward the water, all the while threading his way through flak. Once aboard *Oriskany*, his Skyhawk revealed more than 140 holes.

By the time he completed his final mission in February 1973, now-Cdr Weichman had flown 625 combat sorties and received five DFCs, a Purple Heart and 50 Air Medals, along with the Silver Star. He ended the war as CO of VA-153, flying A-7s from *Oriskany*. Weichman's mission total was the highest of any naval aviator in the war. Retiring as a captain after accumulating 1040 carrier landings and 8200+ flight hours, he was well-liked and respected throughout the Navy. Denny Weichman died of medical complications on his 60th birthday on 11 March 1995.

Lt Cdr Denis Weichman eventually logged 625 combat missions in South-east Asia – more than any other Naval Aviator. His large size (6 ft 6 in) is apparent as he poses by his A-4 in August 1966 after making his 112th landing aboard *Oriskany*. Weichman wears the ubiquitous two-piece camouflaged fatigues favoured by many CVW-16 aviators in place of the official fire-retardant nomex flightsuits that were then just entering service. He eventually accumulated 1039 carrier landings, with 1040 launches – he was shot down once!

NEW SKYHAWK JOINS THE BATTLE

The A-4F had recently deployed with two of *Ticonderoga's* three 'Scooter' squadrons in late 1967. VA-23 and VA-192 were equipped with the upgraded model, and soon other squadrons had transitioned and deployed with the 'Foxtrot'. Characterised by its distinctive dorsal hump, the A-4F featured a more powerful engine, new ejection seat, nosewheel steering – the lack of which had made work harder for flightdeck crews – and avionics installed in a dorsal 'hump'. The new suite included special electronics gear, which was placed atop the fuselage because the jet's premium storage space had been virtually used up in previous years.

Later, the pod was installed on other earlier models, including the A-4E and some A-4Cs, which served exclusively with the reserves as A-4Ls.

TET AND KHE SANH

With all the supplies flowing south, it was obvious something big was in the works. On 30 January, the Viet Cong struck at various points in

South Vietnam – Nha Trang, Pleiku, Da Nang and Qui Nhon. The attacks started a day before the Vietnamese holiday of Tet, marking the lunar new year. The communists even penetrated the American Embassy in Saigon, blasting holes in the protective walls.

While mainly a land battle, with little or no naval air activity, the 1968 Tet Offensive was part of an overall communist attack that by and large failed. The Viet Cong suffered stunning losses, with some estimates at 32,000 dead and 5800 captured in the two-week action. However, farther to the north-west, about six miles from the Laotian border, the embattled camp at Khe Sanh was fighting for its life as thousands of North Vietnamese attacked. The camp was an important block to enemy supplies coming south. It had become obvious to the North Vietnamese that the camp, augmented by Marines in January 1967, had to be taken. Khe Sanh prepared for a major enemy attack.

The 77-day siege of Khe Sanh was a bloody testament to the Marine Corps. The men on the ground fought not only a relentless enemy, but cold, damp weather and supply problems. Ultimately, they prevailed, giving the North Vietnamese a bloody nose they did not forget. Part of the story is the umbrella of air power that included all the services, including several Navy A-4 squadrons.

Lt(jg) John Kuchinski of VA-94 aboard *Bon Homme Richard* flew several missions over the area, coping with the low ceilings and enemy defences that made approaching the camp so hazardous;

'We went every day for about a month to Khe Sanh, with each pilot flying two sorties a day. We checked in with "Waterboy", the controlling agency, who would ask our type and number of aircraft, and what ordnance we had. Then, he'd put us in a stack much like an airliner holding pattern. As flights below you went in, you would drop in altitude and be switched over to a FAC (forward air controller). We were now down to between 11,000-13,000 ft, and the FAC would give us the target, run-in line and location of enemy troops. Then we would salvo all our ordnance on the target and depart. Most of the time you could see where the fire was coming from as you sat in the stack waiting your turn.

'Most of the AAA came from the karst ridges to the north and north-west of the base at Khe Sanh. C-130s would make their approaches from east to west, and most of the flak was directed at them as they landed or dropped off pallets. But sometimes we would take fire as we coordinated our runs with a C-130 approach so as to draw fire away from them.

'I carried a 0.357 Magnum as a personal side arm, and once, as I approached my roll-in point, I had to put negative Gs on the aircraft to avoid tracking flak bursts that were all around me. As I pushed the stick forward, the Magnum came out of its holster on my chest and flew around the cockpit on the lanyard. It hit my helmet and bounced off the canopy a few times. After I rolled in, dropped and departed, I reeled in the pistol and put it back in the holster. Fortunately, I always kept it on an empty chamber for safety, or it might have gone off in the cockpit. Later, I swapped the 0.357 for a little 0.25-calibre automatic.'

Lt(jg) Stephen Gray, who had witnessed Al Crebo's incredible mission on the previous tour, was still with VA-212 aboard 'Bonnie Dick' in 1968. The 'Rampant Raiders' had by now transitioned to the A-4F, along with the 'Blue Blazers' of VA-93. The third A-4 squadron within

Lt(jg) John Kuchinski of VA-94 peers purposefully from his cockpit before flying a mission from the 'Bonnie Dick' during the siege of Khe Sanh

CVW-5, John Kuchinski's VA-94, flew a souped-up version of the A-4E with a more powerful engine that featured 1200 lbs more thrust.

Each Skyhawk usually carried eight bombs – six 500-lb and two 250-lb bombs – along with a 400-gallon fuel tank on the fuselage centreline. As the A-4F carried a dorsal avionics pack, its load of 20 mm ammunition had been restored to 200 rounds per gun.

'Although the smallest and lightest jet on board', Gray recalls, 'the A-4F took the hardest cat shot. Our minimum flying speed off the cat at combat launch weights was 174 knots, which had to be delivered in just 300 ft of catapult stroke. Having the cat set to the proper launch weight was critical'.

Typically, the weather was terrible. On 7 March, the strike force launched then turned south-west and climbed through the clouds toward the coast. Gray's flight leader on this mission was Lt Cdr T R Swartz of MiG killing fame – he had joined the 'Raiders' during cruise work-ups. Flying A-4F BuNo 154092, Gray watched as several more A-4s popped through the heavy clouds and joined up.

The airborne controller known as 'Hillsborough' in an orbiting Air Force C-130 sent the strike force toward Khe Sanh, where they entered a racetrack pattern to await further assignment by the FAC monitoring the action on the ground. Gray and his friends watched as a C-123 cargo aeroplane taxied to take-off position at the end of the runway. It was going to evacuate wounded Marines to Da Nang. Gray recalled;

'Suddenly, I saw a white flash where the wings of the C-123 crossed the fuselage, followed by a yellow blossom of gasoline fire engulfing the entire aeroplane. A mortar round had nailed the transport, and although it was impossible to distinguish people from that altitude, we were sure no one could have survived that explosion. FACs and aircraft below us desperately tried to locate the mortar, but the NVA regulars were experienced jungle fighters, and experts at camouflage. Finally, we were assigned a FAC who marked trenches with a white phosphorous rocket.'

The A-4s descended to 9000 ft under the USAF FAC's control and dropped their Mk 81 250-lb bombs – the impact points were as close as 100 metres from the base perimeter. The FAC's 'attaboys' did little to relieve the frustration at not being able to see the NVA as they bombed them. Swartz reassembled his division and returned to the carrier.

In the coming weeks, CVW-5's A-4s provided cover for C-130s delivering supplies to Khe Sanh. They knew where the NVA troops were – on the high ground south and west of the base, where they could sweep open ground around the airstrip with rifle and mortar fire. Retrieving supplies from the C-130s was extremely dangerous.

On 10 March the runway was closed, and the A-4s were again

Heading back to 'Bonnie Dick' in early 1968, five (including the cameraship) F-model Skyhawks from VA-212 fly in very loose formation. Note that these aircraft all have their tailhooks extended (*via John Kuchinski*)

BATTLES AND BOMBING HALTS

circling above the embattled camp. They were waiting to do a Combat Sky Spot drop, which was a radar-directed bomb dump over a specific area. Stephen Gray, who was flying A-4F BuNo 154174, recalled;

'We would fly at high altitude and simply drop our bombs on command from the radar operator controller. Suddenly, the "Hillsborough" controller called with a contact – a Marine FAC attached to a company on a hill top west of the base. They were coming under heavy fire from a large NVA force and needed CAS immediately.

'Normally, Marine CAS was the province of Marine units, but none were available. The FAC suggested dropping our bombs using a Snakeye delivery because we could make only one pass, and fuel was a concern. The delivery involved a shallow ten-degree dive and releasing the bombs 800 ft above the target.'

A bow-on view of *Bon Homme Richard* underway in the South China Sea in 1968. The vessel spent 135 days on the line between February and September of that year, completing its fourth of six war cruises on 10 October when it returned home to Alameda, California. Commissioned on 26 November 1944, the 'Bonnie Dick' gave the Navy almost 30 years of service. Decommissioned on 2 July 1971 and made part of the Reserve Fleet at Bremerton, Washington, the aircraft carrier was eventually sold for scrapping in March 1992 (*PH1 D I Peth*)

The pilots selected a switch on their bombing consoles that pulled off the bands holding the folding fins of the Snakeye bombs, allowing the fins to deploy *after* they had left the aircraft.

'It was an extremely accurate bomb delivery, but one we didn't use very often in North Vietnam because of the intensity of the low-altitude AAA around most targets. But it was perfect for CAS.'

Gray and his flight saw that the Marines had marked their position with red panels and red smoke – there was only 75 metres of clear ground between them and their attackers. The A-4s split into two sections, making a wide sweep south.

'Flashing over the battle, I saw lead and his wingman drop their bombs. I felt my aeroplane jump as my release sequencer rippled the bombs off my wings. Although I couldn't look back to see the results, the relief was evident in the Marine FAC's voice as he gleefully described our bombs hitting the enemy concentration directly. Another FAC gave us a body count of at least 50, with more in the trees.'

When the siege of Khe Sanh was lifted in April, President Johnson called for one of his bombing halts, this time including the area of Hanoi and Haiphong. These incredibly ill-advised tests of North Vietnam's willingness to negotiate were a sad and frustrating indication of just how deep was Washington's misunderstanding of how to run the war, and US airmen were paying for this ignorance with their lives. It was at this time, too, that Johnson declared he would not seek another term as president.

The real shame was that the North Vietnamese were hurting, as *Rolling Thunder* had at last begun to take effect. Had Johnson continued the cycle of heavy strikes on major supply centres and industrial areas, would

the communists have come to the bargaining table? Instead, they now had time to rebuild, reinforce and reassess. As VAdm Cagle wrote in 1972:

'The 37-month effort had cost TF 77 over 300 aeroplanes destroyed in combat over North Vietnam, 1000 others damaged, 83 pilots and crewmen killed, 200 captured and missing. What had it accomplished?

'The damage to the enemy had certainly been heavy. His transportation system, roads, rail lines and bridges had been wrecked. His above-ground fuel system had been severely damaged. His airfields and his air force had been rendered ineffective. His military complexes had been devastated. In 37 months the enemy had not won a major ground battle. He had certainly not succeeded in subjugating South Vietnam by force. On the other hand, we had not forced him to halt his aggression.'

In the end, his words were a hard assessment of what the difficult bombing campaign had not accomplished. Indeed, even though there were many goals unattained, *Rolling Thunder* began to slowly grind to a halt. The initial determination to see the war through to a favourable conclusion had slowly begun to erode. Now, Washington was seriously considering how to get the South Vietnamese more involved, in fact how to literally give the war back to them and extricate American troops and American honour.

Meanwhile, the carrier air wings were evolving. As noted, the A-7 Corsair II quickly established itself as the replacement for both the A-1 – which had been prohibited from going into North Vietnam because of its slow speed and increased enemy defences – and the A-4. When *Coral Sea* returned home in 1968, it brought back the last squadron of single-seat A-1s to make a combat deployment. And the A-4's coverage was also reduced. Even the veteran *Ticonderoga* included only one A-4 unit (VA-112) when it next deployed in February 1969.

However, the strikes did continue, albeit mainly in the panhandle of North Vietnam, and so did the losses. VA-144's Lt Cdr Robert Saavedra was killed on 27 April as he rolled in against enemy trucks. There had been flak in the area, and his wingman reported seeing a large flash, but it could not be definitely determined if Saavedra had been shot down (in A-4E BuNo 151070) or simply flown into the ground.

Lt Cdr Paul W Paine was flying his A-4F (BuNo154214) on 7 May as part of a RESCAP during the rescue of a VF-92 crew who had been shot down by a MiG-21. After the rescue, the supporting aircraft returned to *Enterprise*. As he set up for a second approach following a foul-deck wave-off, Lt Cdr Paine's aircraft pitched nose down. The VA-113 aviator ejected, but was outside the seat envelope and he was killed.

The following day, VA-56's Lt D A Lawrence had to eject from his A-4E (BuNo 152005) after it was hit by ground fire. An SH-3 went some 20 miles inland to retrieve him.

In this fascinating view, two VA-94 A-4Es are being moved to the bow after recovering from a mission on 6 April 1968 (note the director with his arms raised right at the bow). A VF-53 F-8E has preceded the Skyhawks – Crusaders usually recovered first – and is already chained to the deck. The action is probably going to continue with rearming the A-4s for another sortie, as there are two Mk 82 500-lb bombs on dollys in the middle of the crowd of deck crewmen. More will follow as the rest of the aircraft make their way up the flightdeck from the recovery area. A photograph of BuNo 149993 (in the foreground of this shot) is also featured on page 16 (*PH1 Donald Grantham*)

VA-93 lost two aircraft in May. First, Lt(jg) Barry Karger flew into the ground while attacking a bridge near the coast on 14 May. Then, Lt(jg) J A Douglass had to punch out after taking hits during another bridge strike on 21 May. He survived the ejection and was rescued by an SH-3.

VA-212's Lt Cdr R S Thomas was on an *Iron Hand* mission on 21 May but was redirected to provide possible RESCAP services. Flak set his A-4F (BuNo 154974) on fire, and he ejected to be picked up by helicopter. VA-212 lost another A-4F (BuNo 154174) when Lt J E Killian survived his ejection during the 30 May strike against oil tanks north-west of Vinh.

A full two weeks would pass before another Navy Skyhawk went down. This time, it was a VA-56 'Echo' on 15 June. Pilot Lt J M Wright was heading for his target when he felt small arms fire strike his jet (BuNo 149665). As his oil pressure dropped he headed for the water, ejecting when his engine seized. He was soon rescued and returned to *Enterprise.*

The thrust of the daily schedule was no longer the harrowing drives up to Hanoi and Haiphong, with their intense corridors of flak and SAM batteries waiting along the dykes, the rivers and beside the bridges and buildings. Still, there was danger in the southern part of North Vietnam, and in Laos, covered with jungle that protected the vital route of the Ho Chi Minh Trail, and its constant flow of supplies run by determined men and women on anything that moved and could carry a burden. The war was turning from one of hitting industrial complexes to interdicting trucks and carts furtively scurrying along ill-defined, rut-covered paths.

It was a bitter pill to swallow but the truth was that North Vietnam was winning its waiting game. The professed determination that President Johnson had so forcefully enunciated after the Gulf of Tonkin Incidents and for most of the *Rolling Thunder* campaign was gradually eroding, although not because of any lack of skill and dedication from the aircrews that flew from carriers or from shore bases throughout South Vietnam and Thailand.

During the summer and early autumn of 1968, carrier strikes continued, although at a reduced rate. Losses among the air wings also continued, and the A-4 squadrons, although reduced in number, still suffered the occasional loss. VA-55 and VA-105 lost aircraft on 23 September, for example. Lt Cdr Dale Osborne became a PoW when he ejected from his A-4F (BuNo 155015) while attacking river barges with Zuni rockets. A round of 37 mm flak hit his Skyhawk, badly injuring the VA-55 aviator in the left leg and knocking him temporarily unconscious. When he

An interesting two-level perspective of deck operations aboard *Intrepid* in 1968. While a bombed-up 'humped' A-4E of VA-106 receives attention on the flightdeck above, groundcrew manhandle A-4C BuNo 148528 of VA-36 off the elevator into the hangar bay. Both units were in the process of making their second, and last, war cruises when this photograph was taken. The 'Roadrunners' jet was subsequently sold to the Republic of Singapore Air Force in 1980 and rebuilt as an A-4S

63

came to, he could not control the A-4 and punched out. His comrades in prison helped him regain his health to an extent.

Osborne had been one of the cadre of S-2 Tracker pilots that had made the transition to jet light-attack aviation. Already seasoned carrier aviators, they made a large contribution to the overall effort of TF 77.

VA-55 lost another jet on 27 September when Lt D J Wright's A-4F (BuNo 155011) took a 37 mm round in the fuel tank. As Wright crossed the coast, his engine cut out and he ejected, to be picked up by an SH-3.

Only one more Navy Skyhawk had been lost by the end of October. VA-164 A-4E BuNo 151126, flown by squadron XO Cdr Don Erwin, was struck by 85 mm flak. With his aircraft beginning to burn, Erwin tried in vain to jettison his bombs as he headed for the water. Sadly, as he ejected, the aircraft exploded. Either killed or stunned, he did not surface after landing in the water and was probably retrieved by one of the numerous small fishing boats that always dotted the coastal waters of Vietnam. His remains were returned in 1990.

ROLLING THUNDER ENDS

By the end of October 1968, the US government had played out its hand in Vietnam. Numerous operations on the ground and in the air had done nothing to weaken North Vietnam's resolve. There was little to show for all the men who had died, for all the aircraft lost and for the servicemen incarcerated as PoWs in unbearable conditions. In US cities, and in cities around the world, opinion had long ago turned against the war. Political fortunes had risen and fallen in the preceding three-and-a-half years, not the least of which were those of President Lyndon Johnson.

Disheartened by the continuing demonstrations against his policies and the lack of support for continued strategic operations, he called a unilateral halt to bombing operations north of the 17th parallel that divided the two Vietnams. It would take effect on 1 November.

In the 44 months of *Rolling Thunder*, some 900 aircraft had been lost to the expanding network of enemy defences that now included 8000 flak batteries, 150 MiGs and 40 SAM sites. 'Big deck' carriers like *Enterprise*, *Kitty Hawk*, *Ranger* and *Constellation* had seen the last of the faithful 'Scooter' by late 1968. By the end of 1970, only *Hancock* was still flying A-4s. But there was still a lot of action ahead for the Skyhawk, and it would continue to serve until the end of the war.

For the Navy A-4 units, the months that followed the end of *Rolling Thunder* were a time of re-evaluation and planning. The war turned more directly to interdicting the supply flow south along the Ho Chi Minh Trail, named for the folk-hero leader of North Vietnam, who died unexpectedly in September 1969. The previous missions of industrial strikes changed to a cat-and-mouse game of bombing trees and truck parks.

Configured as a tanker, another VA-106 'Echo' (BuNo 152091) heads for the catapult. Note replacement arresting cables in the foreground. These vital elements of the landing operation received constant and rigorous inspection. VA-106 lost two A-4s during the course of its 1968-69 deployment, and the first of these was in fact this very jet. On 23 September 1968, Lt Cdr David Callaghan was conducting a post-maintenance test flight in the aircraft over the Gulf of Tonkin when the Skyhawk's generator failed. He radioed CVS-11 that he was immediately returning to the ship, and set the ailing A-4 up for a long straight approach. Just seconds before touching down, the jet started to bank to the left. Callaghan was unable to stop the aircraft's nose from dropping and the A-4 struck the LSO platform and then plunged into the sea. The pilot did not survive the crash

1
A-4C BuNo 148609/AJ 414 of VA-12, USS *Shangri-la*, 1970

2
A-4F BuNo 154217/NF 306 of VA-22, USS *Bon Homme Richard*, 1969

3
A-4E BuNo 151168/NE 346 of VA-23, USS *Coral Sea*, 1966

4
A-4C BuNo 148528/AK 512 of VA-36, USS *Intrepid*, 1968

5
A-4F BuNo 155008/NP 510 of VA-55, USS *Hancock*, April 1972

6
A-4C BuNo 149497/NG 401 of VA-56, USS *Enterprise*, 1967

7
A-4C BuNo 145122/AK 301 of VA-66, USS *Intrepid*, 1969

8
A-4E BuNo 149993/AG 303 of VA-72, USS *Independence*, 1965

9
A-4C BuNo 147843/NP 684 of VA-76, USS *Bon Homme Richard*, May 1967

10
A-4E BuNo 151105/NF 313 of VA-93, USS *Hancock*, May 1967

11
A-4C BuNo 149538/NF 414 of VA-94, USS *Bon Homme Richard*, 1967

12
A-4E BuNo 152070/AK 216 of VA-106, USS *Intrepid*, 1968

13
A-4C BuNo 147721/NH 401 of VA-112, USS *Kitty Hawk*, 1968

14
A-4C BuNo 147847/NG 301 of VA-113, USS *Enterprise*, 1966

15
A-4E BuNo 152029/NF 503 of VA-144, USS *Bon Homme Richard*, 1969

16
A-4C BuNo 147836/NK 601 of VA-146, USS *Constellation*, July 1967

17
A-4C BuNo 149574/NL 306 of VA-153, USS *Coral Sea*, 1965

18
A-4E BuNo 151054/NL 504 of VA-155, USS *Constellation*, 1966

19
A-4E BuNo 151191/AH 307 of VA-163, USS *Oriskany*, August 1967

20
A-4F BuNo 155022/NP 401 of VA-164, USS *Hancock*, September 1969

21
TA-4F BuNo 153491/NP 416 of VA-164, USS *Hancock*, 1972

22
A-4C BuNo 149621/AJ 300 of VA-172, USS *Shangri-la*, 1970

23
A-4E BuNo 151073/NM 208 of VA-192, USS *Ticonderoga*, April 1967

24
A-4E BuNo 151113/NP 223 of VA-212, USS *Bon Homme Richard*, March 1967

25
A-4C BuNo 148505/NL 616 of VA-216, USS *Coral Sea*, 1968

26
A-4B BuNo 142687/AK 111 of VSF-3, USS *Intrepid*, 1967

27
TA-4F BuNo 153491/TM 00 of H&MS-11, Da Nang, 1969

28
A-4E BuNo 151050/VK 11 of VMA-121, Chu Lai, 1966

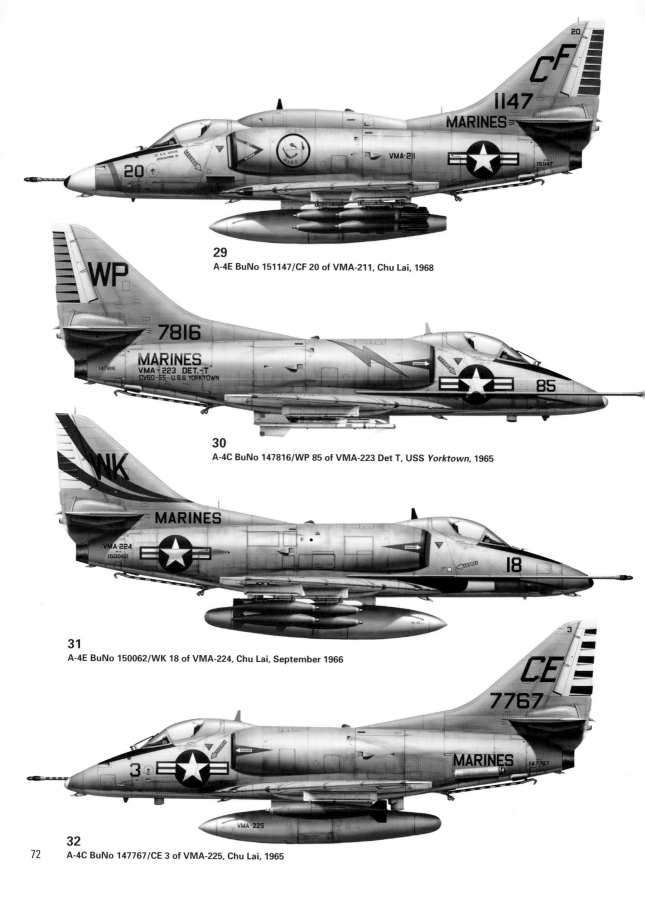

29
A-4E BuNo 151147/CF 20 of VMA-211, Chu Lai, 1968

30
A-4C BuNo 147816/WP 85 of VMA-223 Det T, USS *Yorktown*, 1965

31
A-4E BuNo 150062/WK 18 of VMA-224, Chu Lai, September 1966

32
A-4C BuNo 147767/CE 3 of VMA-225, Chu Lai, 1965

1

2

3

4

5

6

7

8

9

10

11

12

13

THE MARINES

The relationship between the Marine Corps and the A-4 Skyhawk was as long and involved as that of the Navy. VMA-224 was the first Marine A-4 unit, receiving its A-4As in December 1956 – barely four months after VA-72 had became the first Navy squadron to fly it. The A-4M, too late for Vietnam service, was the last production model for American use, and it was made especially for the Marines.

By the time of the Tonkin Gulf Incidents in August 1964, the Marines had gained a lot of experience with the A-4, even flying occasionally aboard carriers. Although the Marines were no strangers to South-east Asia, their presence was somewhat slow to build compared with that of the Navy. Marine Corps UH-34Ds had been operating in South Vietnam since 1962, but Marine fixed-wing aviation took time to arrive.

F-4B Phantom II squadrons and support units with EF-10B Skyknight ECM jets and RF-8A photo-reconnaissance aircraft flew into Da Nang in April 1965. Marine RF-8As had been serving aboard Seventh Fleet carriers in a flying circus arrangement following the events of August 1964 (see Osprey *Combat Aircraft 12 - RF-8 Crusader Units Over Cuba and Vietnam* for further details).

By mid-1965, the 1st Marine Aircraft Wing (MAW) included four Marine Aircraft Groups – MAG-11 had the F-4s, EF-10s, RF-8s and late-arriving F-8s, MAG-16 and MAG-36 were helicopter groups, while MAG-12 eventually included all the A-4 units (except for the HQ squadron H&MS-11 with MAG-11). Meanwhile, the infantry of both the Marines and Army, not to mention that of the Army of the Republic of Vietnam (ARVN), were encountering stiffer engagements. The big F-4s were thirsty and costly to operate at lower altitude where close air support (CAS) was the *raison d'etre* of Marine Corps aviation.

The A-4s were the last to arrive. Space was limited at Da Nang Air Force Base, near Saigon. A new airfield dedicated to the Marines had to be built. Chu Lai, about 55 miles south of Da Nang, was selected. It would include a short airfield for tactical support (SATS) installation – basically a shore-based catapult similar to the well-known launching devices found on carriers. The construction of a SATS installation was no mean feat, given the unstable ground and tendency of the field to turn to mush in heavy rain.

After a colourful, but ultimately unnecessary traditional amphibious landing on 7 May 1965, led by Brig Gen Marion Carl (one of the Corps' top World War 2 aces), construc-

The Marines arrive at Chu Lai on 1 June 1965. With A-4C BuNo 147779 in the background, VMA-225 officers and men cluster around Col John Noble, CO of MAG-12 (bare-headed, rear row), to hear his welcoming remarks. Noble had just flown in with the first aircraft to land at the partially completed airfield. BuNo 147779 was yet another surplus C-model Skyhawk supplied to the Republic of Singapore Air Force in 1980 and rebuilt as an A-4S. It was subsequently upgraded into a Super Skyhawk in the late 1980s by Singapore Aircraft Industries, and the jet remains in frontline service today with the A-4 training unit No 150 Sqn, based at Cazeux, in France. This unit is due to retire its last Super Skyhawks in late 2007 (*Dan Yates*)

tion began. By 31 May, Navy Seebees had built a 4000-ft runway and installed arresting gear. Shortly after 0800 hrs on 1 June, Col John D Noble, CO of MAG-12, brought A-4Cs from VMA-225 to their new home. VMA-311 soon followed with A-4Es. That afternoon, Lt Col Robert W Baker, CO of VMA-225, led his pilots on their first missions.

Rain turned the unfinished field into a sea of mud, and the A-4s had to take off using JATO (jet-assisted take off) bottles and refuel in the air from orbiting KC-130s. Although the runway had a length of 8000 ft, the original material used was not working out, so the Marines decided to use only the last 4000 ft and redo the other half. Eventually, Chu Lai boasted a 10,000-ft strip that could accommodate the heavier, more powerful F-4.

Retired Col Ned Carroll was a major with VMA-121 during its 1966-67 deployment to Chu Lai. He recalled take-offs and landings at Chu Lai;

'Because of an engineering fluke, the bed material for the fabricated aluminium panel that made up the expeditionary runway had been laid over what we thought was laterite rock. However, once the monsoon arrived, we quickly learned that what we had presumed to be rock was actually clay! Softened by the heavy rains, the bedding material soon began to shoot out between the planks every time an aircraft passed over them. Deep voids quickly formed, which made take-offs an adventure, with bumps so bad that eventually bombs were jarred loose and rolled down the runway! These bombs still had safeing wires through their fuses, so there was no immediate danger of them exploding. Still, aircraft-bomb collision, with disastrous results, was always possible.

'This situation required that one half of the 8000-ft strip be shut down to allow re-levelling with a different bed material.

'A 4000-ft runway left little margin for error for an A-4 carrying ordnance. We began using JATO delivered by LSTs to the naval facility just north of Chu Lai. Our Skyhawk squadrons used up the bottles as fast as they were brought in. Pilots would taxi out to the end of the runway for their JATO bottles to be armed, along with the rest of their ordnance. Upon receiving clearance from the tower, and having taxied into position for take-off, we would run the engine up and release the brakes. At 80 knots, we activated the bottles by depressing a button on the catapult brace handle in front of the throttle. We immediately felt the added thrust as the JATO kicked in.

'Nevertheless, we were trained to look up at the two mirrors mounted on the canopy bow. If we could see a blue exhaust in each mirror, we knew things were fine. But if we saw only one exhaust, especially if we were carrying a heavy load, we had to think about ejecting because one bottle would not provide the thrust we needed to take off before reaching the end of the runway.

'After take-off, we climbed out over the water at 250 knots and jettisoned the expended bottles in a designated drop area. When we

A-4C BuNo 147767 of VMA-225 launches with JATO from the half-finished runway at Chu Lai in 1965. The jet carries a minimal load of two Mk 82s and a centreline fuel tank. This aircraft was the second of two Skyhawks lost in non-fatal take-off accidents at Chu Lai on 1 October 1968. By then assigned to VMA-223, the jet had a mainwheel tyre blow and separate from its hub as 1Lt David Habermacher was accelerating down the runway. The A-4 swerved and struck an arrestor gear engine and a revetment before settling back onto the runway, at which point the pilot ejected. Seconds later the Skyhawk crashed and exploded (*Bob Paul*)

returned, we "trapped" in the M-21 arresting gear about 1000 ft down the runway from the normal touchdown point.'

Any surprise the Viet Cong had felt with the arrival of Marine air power was quickly replaced by aggressive battles around Da Nang, which culminated in Operation *Starlite* beginning on 18 July. For a week, Skyhawks and Phantom IIs flew day and night in support of Marines on the ground. By the 24th, the enemy had been contained and pushed off, and Da Nang and Chu Lai remained in American hands.

There were two types of missions for the A-4 squadrons now stationed in South Vietnam – pre-planned and on-call. The grunts would submit a request for CAS the afternoon before their operation, and the Direct Air Support Center (DASC) and Tactical Air Direction Center (TADC) at Da Nang would coordinate the arrangements. The MAG would schedule flights and assign squadron responsibilities for the missions next day.

The on-call missions were more spontaneous, being launched when a ground unit was in contact with enemy forces or when targets of opportunity appeared. Marine ground units were not the only recipients of VMA CAS. In June 1965, the MAG-12 A-4s, in company with MAG-11 F-4s, harassed communist rebels attacking a government outpost at Ba Gia, just 20 miles south of Chu Lai. In October and November, US Army and ARVN troops also required Marine A-4s at Plei Me – the Skyhawks making their first night launch – and at the big engagement in the Ia Drang Valley against some 6000 enemy troops.

As 1965 progressed, the Marine squadrons found themselves in demand by other services, and occasionally accompanied the main Navy or Air Force strike groups into North Vietnam. In December, aircraft from MAG-11 and MAG-12 struck communist supply routes in Laos along with Navy and Air Force missions, flying nearly 300 sorties in three weeks. The strikes were not without losses.

On 29 December, 1Lt Thomas F Eldridge of VMA-211 was escorting helicopters in A-4E BuNo 150019. His squadron had arrived in October as the fourth Marine A-4 squadron in-country. The Marines's first combat loss of a Skyhawk occurred as Eldridge began his attack against enemy positions threatening helicopters bringing supplies to a beleaguered ARVN position south of Chu Lai. Ground fire hit the A-4, wounding the young pilot, who tried to bring himself and his jet back to Chu Lai. However, he crashed 20 miles south of the field and was killed.

A rotation arrangement allowed other squadrons to relieve the original units. VMA-224's A-4Es relieved VMA-225 on 29 September and VMA-223 relieved VMA-311 on 14 December. By the end of 1965, MAG-12 consisted of VMA-211, VMA-214, VMA-223 and VMA-224.

VMA-214 suffered several damaged aircraft during this period, beginning on 27 June when the pilot of A-4C BuNo148553 took small arms fire and tried to eject. However, his seat would not fire and he was able to make it back to Chu Lai for an arrested landing without flaps. Other 'Black Sheep' jets came back with damage ranging from small-arms bullet holes to flak-shrapnel gouges that required greater repair effort.

VMA-224 and VMA-225 also had their share of in-flight damage with four 'Bengal' (VMA-224) A-4Cs returning on 10 May with strikes. In fact, while the Navy's carrier air wings were certainly experiencing their own baptism of fire, the newly arrived Marine Corps squadrons were also

A groundcrewman refuels A-4C BuNo 148465 from VMA-225 through its aerial refuelling probe – a rather unusual, but expedient, method! This aircraft, photographed here in June 1965, was also supplied to the Republic of Singapore Air Force in 1980

going through their own dangerous initiations.

Earlier in December, MAG-12 A-4s hit targets in Laos for the first time, striking enemy infiltration and supply routes as part of the *Steel Tiger* programme. By this time the monsoon season had begun, turning fields into mud. Even the SATS system at Chu Lai was hard pressed, requiring constant maintenance and renovation. From 25 to 27 November, all missions were cancelled because of the heavy rains, high winds and low ceilings.

Adding to the Marines' problems was salt water contamination of the fuel supply, as well as ordnance shortages. 1st MAW issued an order requiring unused ordnance be brought back.

1966

When the SATS became fully operational, seven Skyhawk squadrons rotated in and out of the base, constantly on alert, if not airborne. The importance of the Skyhawk VMAs required keeping the squadrons continuously at Chu Lai and rotating people and aircraft on an individual basis. This arrangement allowed continuous operation, without the unavoidable disruption caused by replacing entire squadrons.

In January 1966, 1st MAW was spread out all over South Vietnam. Its aircraft ranged up and down the Indochina peninsula, participating in every capacity from close air support to cargo-hauling and strategic strikes in concert with other US military services. But, of course, the fixed-wing jets' main responsibility was supporting the troops in the field.

On 3 February, VMA-223 set a record for a day's sorties, flying 59 missions. On 29 April, Capt William F Mullen of VMA-223 was killed during a strike near the Ban Karai Pass – a particularly dangerous area in Laos, where the enemy had established a very active collection of light flak nests that put up a lot of fire. Flying A-4E BuNo 151047, Capt Mullen was on his first pass when his aircraft was hit and caught fire. It was the 'Bulldogs'' first combat loss.

On 16 June, Capt Lynn A Hale took his two-aeroplane section to help a Marine platoon pinned down by a group of NVA regulars. Threading their way through the mountainous area in early morning light, and in the face of heavy enemy fire, the section made repeated runs with bombs and 20 mm cannon. Having expended their weapons, the two A-4 pilots flew back to Chu Lai to refuel and rearm. Then they took off and returned to the same area. Hale received the DFC for his determined support of his fellow Marines on the ground.

Operations for VMA-223 continued to be intense through October and November. In December, the unit returned to Japan to rest and regroup.

Another hard-working Skyhawk unit was VMA-311 'Tomcats', which eventually accrued some 50,000 sorties during the war. Indeed, it was

Led by an A-6A Intruder of VMA(AW)-533, three A-4Es from VMA-311 head toward their target on a partially overcast day. Cloud cover provided the enemy with little respite from the Marine Corps' fighter-bombers thanks to TPQ-10 radar, which involved ground-based radar and computers guiding receiver-equipped Phantom IIs, Skyhawks, and later Crusaders, to specific areas and telling the pilots when to release their bombs. In rain and low clouds, which constantly made such missions more difficult, the TPQ-10 set-up proved its worth as operations began to accelerate once Chu Lai was fully operational. The A-4E closest to the camera (BuNo 151038) survived its frontline service in Vietnam and was subsequently upgraded with an avionics 'hump' and passed on to Marine reserve unit VMA-131 in the mid 1970s. By the late 1980s the aircraft had been stripped of much of its avionics and both of its 20 mm cannon and transferred to fleet adversary unit VF-45 at NAS Key West. The Skyhawk was eventually retired to the Aerospace Maintenance & Regeneration Center (AMARC) at Davis-Monthan AFB on 22 June 1994, and it sat here until acquired by the Yanks Air Museum of Chino, California, on 17 July 2001

among the first to arrive and the last to leave in 1973. VMA-311 had been active during *Starlite*, when the VC tried to overrun Chu Lai in August 1965, and 'Tomcat' pilots flew in support of ground units in the vicious fighting in the A Shau Valley in March 1966. It was during this engagement, that the first VMA-311 pilot was lost. 1Lt Augusto M Xavier was flying an early morning support mission in the pre-dawn darkness when he struck a mountain while strafing NVA troops. He received a posthumous Silver Star for his determination in pressing home the attack.

In July, VMA-311 supported Operation *Hastings*, which was the largest and most profitable Marine Corps operation to date. Besides the large size of the operation, *Hastings* was unique because the enemy was no longer just a few VC guerrillas, but a large division of professional NVA regulars.

By August the squadron had flown more than 7000 combat sorties, involving 10,000 flight hours. Squadron pilots were flying a combined average of 600-700 combat hours a month on what was, quite naturally, dangerous work. The Marine A-4s were hit time and again, but the simple, sturdy construction of Ed Heinemann's little bomber usually allowed heavily damaged aircraft to reach home – but not always.

On 11 May, 1Lt James H Villeponteaux was killed while on a night *Steel Tiger* mission against the Ho Chi Minh Trail in southern Laos. Flying A-4E BuNo 151995, the VMA-311 aviator had a mid-air collision with another 'Tomcat' A-4, which although badly damaged was able to make it back to Chu Lai. Another Tomcat aviator was killed on 6 September. 1Lt Thomas H Hawking, in A-4E BuNo 152020, was supporting US Army troops near Phuc Yen when he struck trees as he pulled out from his attack run. Having ejected and landed safely, the aviator seemed to be on his way to a 'routine' rescue as an Army UH-1 approached dangling a rescue sling. Hawking got into the sling, but as the helicopter rose, he slipped out of the makeshift hoist and fell 1000 ft to the jungle below.

VMA-224's 1Lt Richard M Bloom died two weeks later when his A-4E (BuNo 150054) took hits and burst into flames. At low altitude, and with possible wounds, the pilot did not eject and the A-4 crashed.

Capt Claude N Williams of VMA-223 was killed on the night of 24/25 November. Flying A-4E BuNo 151123, he was shot down only seven miles north-west of Chu Lai – a TPQ-10 radar installation was tracking Williams at the time. Possibly hit by enemy ground fire, he was the last Marine Skyhawk pilot to be lost in 1966.

1967 TO 1970

As 1967 dawned, the US involvement in South-east Asia was increasing beyond what even the most hawkish supporters would have guessed two years earlier. There were 280,000 troops in country, 60,000 of whom were Marines, with another 60,000 sailors and Marines aboard the ships of TF 77, along with 35,000 servicemen in Thailand.

Although the Marine Corps was notoriously stingy with awards above the Air Medal, several A-4 pilots nevertheless received at least one DFC during their Vietnam tours. VMA-121's Maj Ned Carroll and his wingman, Maj Fred Anthony, each received the DFC

for a mission on 6 March 1967. The two A-4s were diverted from their assigned mission of helicopter escort to providing CAS for an ARVN patrol that was virtually surrounded by communist Viet Cong insurgents near Quang Ngai, south of Chu Lai. The two A-4s each carried four pods of 2.75-in rockets and 100 rounds of 20 mm ammunition.

Maj Carroll led his section up through a 500-ft overcast and light rain and called the airborne tactical controller, who told him the South Vietnamese were in a small valley, and that the enemy controlled the hills overlooking their position. Finding a hole in the clouds, Maj Carroll and his wingman descended to 1000 ft. The rain and clouds obscured much of the terrain, making flying around the mountain tops extremely hazardous. Carroll began his attack as the TAC(A) – flying a USAF O-1 Bird Dog – marked the target with white phosphorus rockets.

The only approach was on a low-altitude heading toward the mountains, demanding an abrupt break-away after releasing ordnance to avoid hitting the ground. Maj Carroll made his first pass over the target and fired off all four of his rocket pods. Maj Anthony followed with two rocket runs and a strafing pass. Each run received fire from the enemy positions, but the Marine aviators delivered their weapons only 200 metres from the ARVN troops.

The A-4 squadrons were extremely busy supporting the many ground actions day and night, often close to big population centres. MAG-12 now had VMAs -121, -211, -214 and -311 at Chu Lai. On 6 January, Capt M F Adams had to eject from his A-4E (BuNo 150036) while attacking communist troops southwest of Da Nang. The VMA-121 aviator was retrieved by a Marine helicopter. Squadronmate Capt C R Fye had to eject on 14 January. Flying A-4E BuNo 150106, Fye's aircraft was hit by ground fire and began to burn. He, too, was rescued by a Marine helicopter.

Besides the losses, Marines A-4s also took their share of damage, but still returned home. The 'Black Sheep' of VMA-214 recorded several strikes usually from ground fire such as heavy machine guns or light automatic weapons.

VMA-311 had 19 A-4s, and it flew them constantly, racking up 914 hours in January 1967 and attaining its 10,000th combat sortie on the 20th. Unit CO Lt Col Roger A Morris logged his 7000th flight hour during this period. On 4 February, 1Lt Richard N Bloomberg's A-4 was

Laden down with six Mk 82 Snakeye bombs, A-4E BuNo 151999 'VK 17' of VMA-121 gets a final okay from its plane captain at Chu Lai. Transferred to VMA-311 in 1970, this aircraft was written off in an operational crash while flying from MCAS Iwakuni on 6 February 1973 (*Mike Green*)

Then-Maj Ned Carroll of VMA-121 wears his newly awarded DFC on his utilities in March 1967. Decorations such as this were only sparingly presented to Marine Corps aviators in Vietnam

hit by flak while he was attacking enemy positions north of Da Nang. He headed for Da Nang and had to cut off his overheated engine prior to making a dead-stick landing.

THE SIEGE OF KHE SANH

In May 1967, VMAs -121, -211 and -223 lost three aeroplanes and pilots within four days. Four months later, the Marines took over the Army base at Khe Sanh, which was a remote installation in the north-west corner of Quang Tri province just south of the DMZ near the Laotian border. It was a sensitive, strategic area as far as the North Vietnamese were concerned because it was almost right on the Ho Chi Minh Trail, over which so much of the supply effort to VC elements in the south flowed. There was no way Hanoi could allow continued occupation of such an important site. One western writer compared Khe Sanh as the fulcrum of a pole connecting the two 'rice bowls' of North and South Vietnam.

Fighting in the area initially began in April, when Marine patrols clashed with NVA units. The former quickly learned they were up against a well-trained, aggressive enemy, and for three weeks the fighting was unrelenting. For the moment, in mid-May, the NVA seemed to retreat – it had lost 940 men killed, while Marine losses were 155 killed.

During the coming months, the Marines improved their defences, including building a new airstrip away from the dirt and mud of the original strip. The new runway was opened on 27 October.

The enemy's elaborate battle plans saw a big offensive using NVA and VC divisions to engage ARVN and American units all over South Vietnam during the Tet holiday. It was an unsuccessful campaign from Hanoi's viewpoint, as no territory was captured and the communists lost 32,000 fighters killed and 5800 captured.

However, farther to the north-west, the Marines were once again fighting for their lives at Khe Sanh. Beginning on 21 January 1968, the communists shelled the embattled base almost daily and sent sapper units in to kill Marines and disable facilities. It was obvious that Hanoi meant this Battle of Khe Sanh to be to the finish. As previously related, air support came from all services, including the Navy and Air Force. And the Marine aircraft groups were in the thick of the fighting, protecting their own.

One development was quickly labelled 'the super gaggle', which was first flown on 24 February. Armed UH-1E Hueys and A-4s would escort as many transport helicopters as could be mustered on any one day. The jets would launch from Chu Lai, while CH-46s would come from Quang Tri and fly to Dong Ha to pick up their supply loads. Under the coordination of two-seat TA-4Fs recently arrived in-theatre, the super gaggle would head toward Khe Sanh.

Under the fearsome umbrella of rockets and napalm delivered by the orbiting A-4s, the transport heli-

A-4E BuNo 150046 of VMA-211 heads out on a mission armed with 'daisy-cutters' – rods screwed into the noses of dumb bombs, which allowed them to detonate 36 inches above the ground and cut a devastating swathe in the blast area. Amongst the first Marine E-models to be fitted with an avionics 'hump', this aircraft joined VMA-214 at MCAS El Toro, California, in early 1970 when the unit finally retired its elderly C-model jets. BuNo 150046's association with the famous 'Black Sheep' was not to last long, however, as the jet was lost in an operational accident on 7 May 1970 (*R Rivers*)

copters – usually CH-46s – would spiral down through the clouds and mist that overspread the Khe Sanh area, deposit their supply loads and take off to head back to Da Nang and Chu Lai. The A-4s took advantage of orbiting KC-130 tankers to refuel and escort the empty helicopters back to safety.

BREAK FOR THE 'PLAYBOYS'

FACs were a World War 2 development that matured in Korea, where they had become airborne in T-6 propeller-driven trainers and other available light aircraft. However, the Marines fine-tuned the concept, using TF-9J Cougars, which had been serving simultaneously as advanced trainers in the Navy's Training Command squadrons in Texas. Two H&MS headquarters squadrons (usually called 'HAMS') had been flying the ageing, but dependable, TF-9s for two years, and it was obvious that a replacement was required.

Douglas had built two TA-4Es, extending the forward fuselage of the basic A-4E to accommodate another cockpit. A production model was ordered and designated TA-4F, using an uprated engine, with deliveries beginning in May 1966. Later, several F-models were modified into TA-4Js, and these, along with purpose-built 'Juliets', entered the Training Command in 1969. The aircraft would subsequently enjoy more than 35 years of service in the Navy's VT training units, and as adversary aircraft in utility VC squadrons.

The first TA-4Fs arrived in Vietnam in August 1967, assigned to H&MS-11 (the headquarters squadron for MAG-11, based at Da Nang). The new aircraft offered good endurance at low level, as well as a variety of armament capabilities – usually two pods of Zuni rockets and 20 mm cannon. Immediately put to work, the two-seaters flew as airborne command posts over Khe Sanh, coordinating the huge stacks of aircraft waiting to spiral down through the clouds and mist to deliver their loads on the enemy. The TA-4Fs also helped the heavy surface ships offshore, calling in fire adjustments for the battleship USS *New Jersey* (BB-61) as it pounded enemy positions with its 16-inch guns.

In June 1969, the TA-4F crews took the call sign 'Playboy', complete with the stylised bunny's head associated with the popular men's magazine of the same name. Indeed, Hugh Hefner, the magazine's dapper publisher, gave them permission to use the logo. MAG-11 and MAG-12 crews, occasionally augmented by 'moonlighting' F-4 crews from VMFA-542, continually flew the hard-working two-seaters.

The big bombing halt of 1 November 1968, which only allowed the enemy to build up his operation and supply flow, increased the burden on Marine ground units. The action was especially busy along the Laotian border – quite naturally the focal point of the entry of supplies into South Vietnam via the Ho Chi Minh Trail. The TA-4Fs' UHF and FM

TA-4F BuNo 153491 is seen between missions at Da Nang in 1968 – note the small Playboy bunny logo near the fin tip, indicating the call sign of H&MS-11. This aircraft eventually wound up aboard *Hancock* assigned to VA-164 in 1972. BuNo 153491 ended its days with Marine Aviation Logistics Squadron (MALS) 24 at MCAS Kaneohe Bay, Hawaii, in the late 1980s. Its final whereabouts remains unrecorded

radios permitted their crews to work with both airborne jets and ground forces.

TA-4F units also ran an exchange programme with the 'Misty' FACs of the Air Force, who were flying F-100 Super Sabres. Marine pilots flew a minimum of five flights in the two-seat F-100F, while USAF pilots did a similar number of missions in the back seat of the TA-4F. Navy crews also took advantage of the opportunity to fly with the Marines, with this exchange serving two purposes – it gave Navy pilots a much better understanding of the overall mission, and it helped the Marine Corps cope with the pilot shortage that plagued it at this time.

The Marines also benefitted from their association with the USAF's rescue forces, such as on 9 April 1969. Maj Robert S Miecznikowski and Capt James C Buffington of H&MS-11 were flying TA-4F BuNo 154299 over Laos when their aircraft was hit by 37 mm flak. Ejecting from their Skyhawk, the two Marines were rescued by an Air Force HH-53. The Super Jolly Greens would pick up two more 'Playboy' crews in coming months.

Former 'Playboy' retired Col Larry Adkinson wrote in the newsletter of the Skyhawk Association;

'We divided the crew duties so that the back-seater observed the road while the front-seater navigated and avoided terrain or weather. Although the enemy threat dictated most of our low altitude manoeuvres, we did our best to maintain the field of vision for the back-seater.

'For example, on 7 July 1969, operating at very low altitudes, "Playboy" spotted/adjusted for a flight of A-6As flying radar offset-aim-point delivery tactics in overcast (600-ft ceiling) conditions. This resulted in the destruction of an enemy truck convoy that was moving under concealment of the low cloud cover – a fact clearly demonstrated by the 35 mm photos taken by the "Playboys".'

A second 'Playboy' Skyhawk went down on 27 December 1969. TA-4F BuNo 154621, flown by Maj Richard E Lewis and 1Lt Paul E Phillips, was on a *Steel Tiger* mission over Laos when it was hit by flak. The two Marine aviators ejected but had to wait overnight before being rescued by an Air Force Jolly Green that came under heavy enemy fire.

A third TA-4 was lost on 11 July 1970 when Capt R T Rasmussen and 1Lt W W Mills ejected from TA-4F BuNo 154646 after being hit by ground fire while marking a target in the A Shau Valley. Again, the Air Force sent in an HH-53, which picked up the Marines under heavy fire. The Jolly Green sustained 15 hits in a six-hour gun battle.

TA-4F BuNo 153506 'TM 2' of H&MS-11 rolls out on the Da Nang runway following a post-maintenance check flight (its back seat is empty) in 1967. Note the Pan Am Boeing B707s in the background. Following many years of service with various Marine Corps HQ units, this aircraft was transferred to fleet adversary unit VF-126 at NAS Miramar, California, in the late 1980s. It served with the 'Bandits' until retired to AMARC on 4 December 1991. On 12 July 2005, BuNo 153506 was one of a pair of two-seat Skyhawks (TA-4J BuNo 158509 was the other aircraft) transferred to NAS Fallon, Nevada, to act as range targets for Navy air wings undertaking pre-deployment training

By the time the 'Playboy' mission was discontinued in September 1970, two crewmen had been killed in action. Lt Col George Ward in March 1970 and Maj Larry Robinson, who had been flying an F-4B of VMFA-542 on 5 January 1970. Robinson and his RIO, 1Lt Robert W Burnes, were escorting a TA-4F on a mission against an enemy flak battery when it opened up and hit the F-4. Neither crewman ejected, which meant that they may have been wounded and incapacitated.

Lt Col Ward and his back-seater, 1Lt Paul Lowery, who flew with H&MS-11 whenever he could get away from his staff job, were on a low-level mission over Laos on 19 March in TA-4F BuNo 154622. They attacked a truck convoy towing SAMs with Zunis. Several enemy soldiers dismounted from their transports and started firing at the Marine jet.

Lt Lowery could hear their bullets hitting his jet and eventually saw blood on the canopy. At this point he noticed that Lt Col Ward was slumped over. As the TA-4 began a roll and was headed for the ground, Lowery quickly realised Ward was not in control, so he grabbed the stick and pulled up. He called the controller in the Air Force C-130 and told him he was heading back to Da Nang, where he made an arrested landing. Col Ward was rushed to the hospital, where he later died of his wounds.

BACK TO KHE SANH

The confrontation over Khe Sanh was far from over. Following the Tet holiday, NVA divisions began bombarding the US enclave. It was the start of one of the most intense engagements of the long war. Foremost among the jet squadrons were the VMAs and their A-4s.

The opening salvoes of enemy artillery on 22 January hit an ammunition dump outside the main camp. Some 6000 Allied troops were matched against an estimated 20,000 NVA. During the two-month siege, a tremendous aerial operation involving supply trains of helicopters and transports ran the gauntlet of communist flak batteries as they approached Khe Sanh's strip to deliver their pallets, sliding the platforms out the rear hatches without touching down. The terrain around the camp soon took on the appearance of a moonscape repainted in brick red.

VMA-311 was especially active supporting the 26th Marines. On 21 January, Capt Bobby Downing ejected from his A-4E (BuNo 151140) during a strafing run. He was rescued by a Marine Huey as his wingman strafed enemy positions.

William F Loftus had seen a lot of action around Khe Sanh the previous year. Now a major, he was flying A-4E BuNo 150053 on 23 January against a communist troop position near Khe Sanh. At 1500 ft, his Skyhawk was hit by ground fire, forcing Loftus to eject near the Marines he was trying to protect. The grunts rushed forward when the newly grounded aviator's parachute shroud lines became entangled in the barbed wire surrounding the base. A helicopter airlifted Loftus back to his squadron at Chu Lai.

The siege of Khe Sanh last 77 days, with the communists not yielding until the second week in April. After some of the hardest and closest combat of the war, the NVA simply faded back into the mists, leaving the scarred pockets of Marines and Army troops to tally the cost.

Besides the heavy fighting at Khe Sanh, there were many other enemy operations during the Tet Lunar New Year holiday – usually a time of celebration and less warlike activities. Tet 1968 became a synonym for the bloodiness of the Vietnam War, and although most communist objectives were thwarted, the cost in American casualties was terrible. Da Nang, Saigon and Chu Lai itself came in for direct attacks.

On 29 January, while on a Tet-related CAS mission south of Da Nang, Capt James D Mills of VMA-211 (in BuNo 149976) was shot down and killed. Another 'Avenger' A-4 (BuNo 150104) was lost on 25 February when Maj V P Hart ejected south of Da Nang after being hit by ground fire. A third VMA-211 Skyhawk went down, this time with the loss of the pilot, on 24 March. Capt Charles W Porterfield took off on a CAS mission, but apparently his A-4E (BuNo 152068) quickly developed a problem which forced it to veer off the runway at Chu Lai and crash.

A TA-4F of the 'Playboy' det was lost on 11 April. MAG-11 CO Col Leroy T Frey and Maj D F Newton survived their ejection after their two-seater (BuNo 153511) was hit during an attack on a communist position near Da Nang.

The squadrons of A-4s rotated in and out, and as each arriving unit began its schedule of sorties, it would lose a concentrated number of aircraft and, occasionally, pilots. VMA-121 had spent a long tour beginning in September 1967. Following Khe Sanh, the 'Green Knights' continued their operations. On 5 May 1968, two of its A-4Es launched from Chu Lai to hit NVA troops up north near Quang Tri. Making his third pass, 1Lt T M Aiton felt his Skyhawk (BuNo 151105) shudder from ground fire. He punched out to be rescued by a Marine helicopter.

Maj L D Tyrell survived his ejection from A-4E BuNo 152092 four days later, bailing out over the water off Da Nang after sustaining damage. Two 'Tomcat' aviators surpassed the 500-mission mark whilst in-theatre – Capt Peter A Kruger in May 1968 and Capt Durwood K Schnell in August 1969 (the latter flew 533 missions in total).

By mid-1969, American dissatisfaction with the war, coming largely from dissidents at home and a new presidential administration headed by Richard M Nixon, had promulgated a disengagement schedule. The US wanted to give the war back to the South Vietnamese. Accordingly, a withdrawal of some 25,000 servicemen was announced on 8 June, followed a year later by an additional 150,000.

In-country assets such as the Marine Corps squadrons at Da Nang and Chu Lai were affected. However, the units that went home were A-6 and F-4 squadrons, as well as one complete helicopter aircraft group. The A-4 units continued their rotating deployments, shuttling back and forth between Japan and South Vietnam. MAG-11 remained, although greatly reduced, to fight the on-going war, for the North Vietnamese had no intention of withdrawing.

Shown in March 1968, each one of these Marine A-4 aviators from VMA-311 received the DFC. They are, from left to right, Maj William F Loftus, Lt Col Richard B Taber, Maj John H Buchanan and Maj Darrell Shelor. Maj Loftus had ejected from his A-4E (BuNo 150053) two months earlier while strafing communist troops near Khe Sanh on 23 January (*LCpl Mike Servais*)

A DOUBTFUL ENDING

The air war in Vietnam changed dramatically following President Johnson's unilateral bombing halt of 1 November 1968. Gone were the massive Alpha strikes that involved two or three strike groups from as many different carriers. Gone, too – or nearly so – were the confrontations between the MiGs and the slashing F-4 escorts and F-8 TAR-

CAPs, trying to protect the struggling A-4 bombers. The air war that evolved from late 1968 was that of concentrated interdiction against the constant flow of supplies to the south that fuelled the enemy's capability to continue fighting in the jungles and paddies around the population centres along the coast. Almost by necessity, the focus shifted from the industrial heartland of North Vietnam to the northern tendrils of the Ho Chi Minh Trail in Laos.

As America sought to reduce its troop count on the ground, it still maintained a regular number of carrier strike groups in the South China Sea. *Hancock* and *Intrepid* gave way to *Coral Sea* and *Ticonderoga*, who left when *Kitty Hawk* and *Ranger* arrived. A dramatic change on the flight decks was the A-4's exodus. Squadrons that had made three or four combat cruises with the veteran 'Scooter' now flew the A-7 Corsair II. Others making their last deployment with the A-4 were scheduled to transition to the A-7. Occasionally, there was a mix of the old and new.

'Tico's' 1969 cruise included two A-7B (the first deployment with this model) squadrons – VA-25 and VA-87 – and lone A-4C squadron VA-112 'Broncos'. Although boasting a three-squadron light-attack capability, CVW-16's modernity was somewhat deceiving. The A-4s' capability was not the same as the new A-7s. This deficiency was no more clearly shown than during the international crisis resulting from the downing of a Navy EC-121 by North Korean fighters on 14 April, with the loss of its 31-man crew.

A-4F BuNo 154217 from VA-22 shows the distinctive dorsal hump that housed avionics and made room for restored ammunition in the fuselage. This photo was taken during the unit's 1969 war cruise. BuNo 154217 is presently on display in the National Museum of Naval Aviation at NAS Pensacola, Florida (*Lt W E Bradford*)

VA-112 pilots wait to start engines for a mission from *Ticonderoga* in 1969. Their elderly A-4Cs struggled to fly with the new A-7Bs from the other two light strike squadrons aboard 'Tico'. Nevertheless, the 'Stallions' gave a good account of themselves (*Fred Ameel*)

The American response was swift, although not as decisive as would be hoped, especially in view of the North Korean high-jacking of USS *Pueblo* (AGER-2) on 23 January 1968 and the internment of its crew until December of that year. Probably emboldened by the lack of US action following the *Pueblo* incident, the North Koreans had

A Skyhawk fires 2.75-in rockets at a target in South Vietnam. These small unguided missiles were used a lot in the first half of the war, but could pose problems for the aircraft that fired them. Indeed, a handful of A-4 pilots had to eject after flying into the field of rockets they had just fired (*via Lou Mortimer*)

tweaked the tail of the 'US tiger' again. TF 71 was reformed, and four carriers and their battle groups were detoured from their normal assignments in the South China Sea to the colder climes off Korea.

CVW-16 was augmented by a third Crusader fighter squadron when VF-51 arrived, taking the place of the RF-8G det of VFP-63. VA-112 was ignominiously sent off to Japan mainly because its A-4Cs were too short-legged to fly with the A-7s. The Skyhawks had been working in South Vietnam at the time, and had seen a fair amount of action, but heading north to an uncertain future, and possible confrontation with a relatively unknown enemy force, was not the time to retain what was becoming an obsolescent aircraft. Predictably, when the crisis eased and TF 71 was reassigned, the A-4s returned to 'Tico' to complete their deployment.

One almost improbable participant in the air war was the old carrier USS *Shangri-la*, now redesignated CVS-38. Commissioned in 1944, it saw action in the Pacific late in World War 2. In and out of mothballs, the 'Shang' usually guarded the vineyards in the Mediterranean. However, the demands on the overall carrier fleet during Vietnam required that the veteran ship make what would be its only combat deployment, carrying CVW-8. The air wing's complement included three A-4 squadrons – VA-12 (A-4C), VA-152 (A-4E) and VA-172 (A-4C).

Shangri-la was not given the affection that usually comes to ageing ships, perhaps because its numerous afflictions and problems left little room for such emotions. Thus, it was with some disbelief that people on and off the carrier saw it sortie from Mayport, Florida, on 5 March 1970, its final destination the South China Sea and the war. System breakdowns, inadequate air conditioning and a general malaise followed the converted CVS, even though its hard-working crew enjoyed what many considered a fine mess and an entertaining movie schedule.

T R Swartz's MiG-killing A-4C BuNo 148609, now assigned to VA-12 and CVW-8 in 1970 for the one combat cruise of *Shangri-la*, departs NAF Atsugi following a short R&R break ashore (*Masaaki Hayakiwa*)

'Shang' eventually checked in on *Yankee Station* on 8 April. CVW-8 soon learned that its main activity would be flying sorties into Laos. The first mission came on 11 April, and involved all three light attack squadrons. The old carrier struggled to keep up speed to provide adequate wind over the deck for launch. The Skyhawks were penalised accordingly, and could only carry three of the normal four 500-lb bombs.

Arriving over their target and directed by an orbiting USAF FAC, the strikers made their run and returned to the carrier, satisfied with having flown their first mission. However, it was not always going to be so easy, and within ten days CVW-8 had lost its first aircraft – A-4C (BuNo 148484) of VA-172, flown by Lt(jg) John B Golz. In fact, this jet proved to be the cruise's only combat loss. On 22 April, Golz was part of a late-night mission sent to attack trail traffic. In the rising dawn light, the FAC watched as Golz's A-4 went into its attack dive and hit the ground. No flak was seen, but the probable cause was considered to be ground fire or pilot target fixation – an ever present danger in such low-level operations.

Shangri-la spent the next eight months on and off the line. Its crews contended with the old ship's operational problems, and pilots dealt with flying obsolescent A-4Cs against a hidden enemy. Yet, Jim Reid, the aircraft handler for the cruise, recalls the deployment with guarded enthusiasm. Despite such aggravating problems as contaminated jet fuel, arresting cables that unravelled, failure of the ship's TACAN directional beacon and a host of other daily and periodic headaches, there were moments of dark humour.

At one point, shortly before Reid's arrival, the carrier's No 3 elevator had been out of commission for three weeks, requiring a new cable that had actually arrived at Da Nang. The frustrated captain proceeded to con his ship right into the harbour to get both the cable and the shipyard workers needed to make the change!

Beginning in late June, three Skyhawks (two from VA-172 and one from VA-12) were lost during catapult shots. Two of the pilots were retrieved while the third was killed. The problem was traced to the fact that the war-weary A-4Cs had gone well past their safety point and the

VA-172's A-4C BuNo 149498 is also seen in the NAF Atsugi pattern in 1970. This unit was also assigned to CVW-8 for 'Shang's' one-time combat cruise. As with most A-4Cs that survived frontline service with the Navy, this aircraft was sold to the Republic of Singapore Air Force in 1980 and rebuilt as A-4S 991. Upgraded to Super Skyhawk specification in the late 1980s, this aircraft served with No 145 Sqn until the unit retired its A-4SUs in March 2005

Shangri-la during its 1970 cruise. The old carrier was plagued by problems with its systems and aircraft throughout the eight-month deployment, but CVW-8 maintained its mission tempo

On 2 July 1970, VA-152's Lt(jg) William Belden suffered brake failure in his A-4E (BuNo 150127) during recovery, and the aircraft veered toward the port catwalk. The 'Shang's' flightdeck chief, Air Bosun Joe Hammond, grabbed a wing to try to bring the aircraft back on deck, but could not keep the jet from moving over the edge. The young pilot ejected, sending a fuselage access panel into the chief's left shoulder. Belden landed 100 yards from the carrier, where he was rescued by the ship's helicopter. The A-4 was recovered from the catwalk and eventually returned to flight status. Chief Hammond was also returned to normal duty. PH3 Keith Gutherie was on duty to back up the regular automatic PLAT camera that filmed flightdeck action, and he took this celebrated sequence of photographs capturing the incident. In late 1973 it was one of 46 E-models transferred to the Israeli Defence Force/Air Force, where it received the serial number 895. This aircraft is presently in war reserve storage at Ovda air base

bridle attachment point below the wings had simply failed. The jets were no longer attached to the catapult during the launch sequence and simply dribbled off the flightdeck without attaining launch speed.

Shangri-la left *Yankee Station* in November and made its way back to the US, where the vessel was quickly decommissioned in June 1971. The veteran carrier languished at the Philadelphia Navy Yard until it was finally scrapped in 1988.

INVASION OF LAOS

Beginning in February 1971, *Lam Son 719* was a more concentrated, formalised effort to halt the supply flow south. ARVN units jumped off from Quang Tri province on 8 February and struck into Laos. However, even with an umbrella of US air power protecting the South Vietnamese, the NVA resistance was stiff, and ultimately the Allied effort, spearheaded by the South Vietnamese accompanied by American forces, was pushed back.

Hancock was on station at the time with CVW-21, which included the last carrier-based Skyhawks in the war. All the remaining A-4 squadrons had either switched to A-7s or been decommissioned. The three units aboard CVA-19 would also be 'decommed' within the next few years, but the need for CVW-21 and *Hancock* was immediate, so the A-4s went out again.

VAs -55, -164 and -212 all flew the definitive A-4F, which probably eased the burden of maintenance for the enlisted members. The jets were largely responsible for attacking enemy trucks, as well as for providing support for the Marines on the ground. There was also the occasional retaliatory strike into southern North Vietnam. Working in conjunction with Air Force FACs in OV-10s, the CVW-21 A-4s operated primarily around the three major passes – Mu Gia, Ban Karai and Ban Raving – on the Laos-Vietnam border, sometimes going into the so-called Laotian Panhandle, which was actually Air Force territory, codenamed *Steel Tiger*.

A representative mission at this time was the mid-afternoon sortie flown by VA-55 on 21 November near Cape Mui Ron. With a 6000-ft ceiling, the A-4 pilots spotted trucks and made an unsuccessful attack, dropping some of their Mk 82 500-lb bombs. Several other runs proved inconclusive, the clouds making a textbook run-in difficult.

With most of their bombs gone, the A-4 pilots were thinking of going home when a call came that another flight had some communist trucks bottled up on a nearby road. The 'Garfish' section found the new target and destroyed several vehicles. Calling 'Winchester' to indicate they had expended all their ordnance, the VA-55 aviators headed back to *Hancock*.

During *Lam Son 719*, *Hancock's* Skyhawks saw considerable action supporting ground operations. In mid-February a flight was called in near Khe Sanh – which had been vacated several years before – but as they approached the area, the A-4 pilots encountered confusion between Air Force aeroplanes and other Navy aircraft as the FAC and ground units called for help. The FAC called for some aircraft to jettison their ordnance. Everyone could hear an Army helicopter crewman on the emergency frequency. His helicopter had been shot down and was rapidly being surrounded by enemy troops. Another helicopter made it through the ground fire but could only pick up four of the first helicopter's crew, leaving the one man on the ground, pleading for more help on the radio. As the pilots of other helicopters keyed their mikes, the sound of their gunners' machine guns could be heard over the air.

The A-4 pilots were desperate to help, and called for the FAC to coordinate a rescue, but there was no reply. With low fuel, the Skyhawk crews dropped their ordnance in a tree line and left. Tired and frustrated, they recovered aboard the *Hancock*.

This period of the war became a trying time for many aircrew, especially those carrier aviators flying into the thick of the fighting in Laos. This is not to say these men did any less of a job, but as intelligent, trained individuals, they naturally wondered how such confusion could possibly win the war. One of VA-55's pilots was Lt Eliot Tozer III. Like many men involved in the conflict, he kept a journal of his experiences;

'The frustration comes on all levels. We fly a limited aircraft, drop limited ordnance on rare targets in a severely limited amount of time. Worst of all, we do all this in a limited and highly unpopular war – the nature of our war on the tactical level cannot be even partially dispelled, however. Our ordnance load is limited to less than two tons. We're in, have time for two runs and we're bingo for either time or fuel.

'All theories aside, what I've got is personal pride pushing against a tangled web of frustration. One of the ways to slice through the webbing and be free, at least for the moment, of almost all frustration is to press the attack home, and while you jink and claw away from all the reaching AAA, hear the FAC call, "Shit hot, two, you got the son of a bitch!"'

VA-55's Lt Eliot Tozer heads for his Skyhawk aboard *Hancock* during the carrier's 1971 war cruise. A determined individual and capable pilot, Tozer was frustrated by not being able to go after more meaningful targets than tree stands hiding truck parks in Laos during this deployment. He was subsequently killed in a flight mishap in RF-8G BuNo 144615 of Reserve-manned VFP-306 on 28 August 1980 whilst flying from *Coral Sea* off the California coast

Carrying a centreline fuel tank and Mk 82 500-lb bombs, A-4F BuNo 154998 of VA-164 is hooked up to *Hancock's* No 1 cat in 1971

'GARFISH', 'GHOSTRIDERS' AND 'RAMPANT RAIDERS'

VA-164 had outlasted its sister squadron VA-163, which had disestablished in July 1971, but had actually been inactive since April 1969. The 'Saints' had seen a lot of action in their four war cruises, and many pilots had not come home. But it remained for VA-164 to carry on aboard *Hancock*.

VA-164's first loss on its sixth combat tour occurred on 26 January 1971, although it was not in combat. Lt(jg) Gerald L Carter

Lt(jg) Denny Sapp of VA-55 finishes his preflight check before getting into his A-4F, chained down to *Hancock's* flightdeck, during the vessel's 1971 war cruise

launched in A-4F BuNo 154980. However, as he moved down the port catapult, his aircraft did not gain flying speed and fell into the water ahead of the ship. The Skyhawk rolled inverted and sank, carrying the 28-year-old pilot from Oregon with it. Reviewing the film that covers every launch and recovery aboard a carrier, investigators discovered that the cable known as the bridle that hooked the aircraft to the catapult had separated, leaving the A-4 to meander down the track barely reaching an estimated 80 knots instead of the required 130 knots – too slow to fly, but too fast to use brakes.

Watching the terrible event unfold before him was Lt(jg) Dennis J Sapp, waiting to move onto *Hancock's* port catapult after Carter cleared the ship. Stunned, Sapp refused the flightdeck crew's direction to move onto the port cat. Instead, he let them move him to the starboard cat and launched without incident.

Sapp was on his second combat deployment, having joined VA-55 in the last few weeks of its 1969-70 cruise. A native of Iowa, he had been commissioned through the Navy's Aviation Officer Candidate School (AOCS) in May 1968 and received his wings in July 1969. Sapp went back out in October 1970 for a nine-month deployment. He would also make a third war cruise in 1972.

The third veteran A-4 unit aboard *Hancock* was VA-212. The 'Rampant Raiders' had seen their fair share of action early in the war, but the 1972 cruise resulted in the loss of both the CO and the XO. Cdr Henry H Strong Jr had taken command the previous December. On 25 May he led a section as part of a larger strike against targets near Vinh, in southern North Vietnam. Vinh was always well defended, and this mission would prove no exception.

The assigned target was in a busy area with a railway line that paralleled the busy Highway 1A, which connected Thanh Hoa, Vinh and Hanoi. In the early evening, Strong and his wingman set up for their attack. Other crews heard him call, 'Rolling in'. Flak quickly blossomed, and soon the other strikers saw an A-4F (BuNo 155045) dive inverted toward the ground. The pilot did not eject. The only missing Skyhawk in the area at the time was that flown by Cdr Strong. Unlike other crews lost over Vietnam, Strong's remains have never been returned by the Vietnamese, and his ultimate fate remains unknown, although it is obvious he was killed in action. He was the second VA-212 CO to be killed during the war, following Homer Smith, who apparently died in captivity.

XO Cdr Frank C Green Jr launched on the night of 9/10 July in A-4F BuNo 154972 for an armed reconnaissance into North Vietnam. He was 50 miles south of Hanoi when he saw the lights of a truck and began his attack. His wingman, Lt Bill Wylie, saw a flash and could not get a response when he called his leader. Cdr Green was never found, and he did not return in 1973 with the PoWs.

Lt Sapp had launched with Lt Chip Drury on an *Iron Hand* mission that same night. They were soon in contact with a SAM site, and Sapp prepared to launch a Shrike. It was the first time he would fire the missile at night, and the flash blinded him temporarily. As he struggled to regain his sight, Sapp and his wingman could hear Cdr Green and Lt Wylie on their mission. Sapp listened as Wylie called in vain for Green. Wylie was low on fuel, and Sapp volunteered to stick around to look for Green.

Both pilots dropped flares but saw nothing on the ground. Even after a few days of flying over the area, Sapp could not find where Cdr Green had gone down. Then, finally, one more try located the crash site. From the appearance of the latter atop a hill, punctuated by a long burn streak, it seemed that the XO had flown into the ground after a low pullout.

NVA INVADES THE SOUTH

The lethargy that had settled over the war in 1970 and part of 1971 had evaporated with the so-called Easter Invasion of South Vietnam in March 1972 by the NVA. The latter had made good use of the time following President Johnson's 1968 bombing halt, preparing a major drive south to capture Saigon and conquer South Vietnam. At first, its offensive seemed unstoppable. Without the massive umbrella of US support, the ARVN struggled to hold ground against the NVA. Washington found itself playing a desperate game of catch-up reminiscent of the early stages of the Korean War in 1950.

Elements of the Air Force and Marine Corps were quickly recalled to South Vietnam, and carrier groups' orders were changed to send more squadrons to the Gulf of Tonkin as quickly as possible. As Washington scrambled, the carriers already on station worked overtime.

April was a particularly busy month for the CVW-21's A-4s. Denny Sapp participated in one of the most celebrated events of the time – the rescue of USAF Lt Col Iceal E Hambleton, who was the only survivor of the six-man crew of an EB-66C shot down on 2 April. Better known as 'Bat 21', Hambleton spent nearly 12 days evading capture as an all-out rescue effort incorporated ground and air elements of the Navy, Air Force, Army and ARVN.

On 12 April, Lt Sapp was leading a flight of A-4s when he responded to a FAC's frantic call for help against an NVA force that was firing at Hambleton and a small band of Navy SEALs that had found him and were trying to lead him to safety. The FAC guided Sapp and his flight onto the target, which were houses on a river bank from which communist snipers were firing. After marking the houses with smoke rockets, the FAC cleared the jets in. With plenty of fuel, the A-4 pilots took their time, making repeated passes, dropping one bomb at a time and eventually destroying the little village and the enemy vantage point.

A few weeks later, Sapp flew two sorties on one day – not especially rare, but each mission resulted in a decoration. On 29 April, he led a division of A-4 SAM suppressors during a large, coordinated air wing strike on two major enemy transshipment points near Vinh. The well-defended target had six SAM sites, as well as concentrations of AAA batteries.

Working closely with the strike leader, Sapp devised a plan that provided the best protection for the strikers. Figuring out a precise positioning schedule, Sapp and his division fired Shrikes against the sites that had already launched SA-2s. At this point, Sapp lost his ordnance system and could not fire a Shrike at the nearest site. He had also lost his radio, and his wingman had to take over flight lead duties. Sapp followed his wingman down through the 23 mm and 37 mm flak and dropped two 500-lb bombs directly on the site, destroying it.

Later, Sapp led three sections of *Iron Hand* A-4s during another Alpha strike near Thanh Hoa, deep into North Vietnam. Again planning how

to best protect the large strike group, Sapp manoeuvred his flight toward a SAM site that had painted them. After firing one Shrike, he saw two SAMs coming for him and he fired his second Shrike at the site, before manoeuvring violently to evade the oncoming missiles. Sapp beat the SAMs and strafed the site, destroying its radar van.

The first mission resulted in an Air Medal – one of 11 individual awards he received, in addition to 28 strike/flight awards – and the second a DFC, which was the first of two Sapp earned during this cruise. He also eventually garnered nine awards of the Navy Commendation Medal – a fairly large number of this particular medal. Sapp remained on cruise until *Hancock* returned in October.

TA-4s IN COMBAT FROM THE FLIGHTDECK

Two TA-4Fs came on board *Hancock* in August 1972. Assigned to VA-164, the two-seaters (BuNos 154325 and 153491) had been transferred from the Marine Corps, with the 'Playboy' FAC mission having been cancelled two years before in September 1970.

As now-retired Adm Stan Arthur later wrote, 'Pilots of VA-164 logged some serious combat time in the two-seat A-4. The A-4 squadrons of CVW-21 had been assigned responsibility for developing expertise in unique types of missions, an example being VA-55's specialisation in the *Iron Hand* mission. VA-164 deployed with its aircraft wired for equipment to facilitate the delivery of laser-guided bombs, and worked on developing tactics for delivery and control of those weapons in a high-threat environment'.

'Ghostrider' CO Cdr Stanley R Arthur had started his naval aviation career flying S-2s, but he had changed to jets as a lieutenant commander. He flew 514 combat missions in Vietnam, accumulating 11 DFCs and 51 Air Medals. Capping off his 38-year career, he rose to four-star rank, serving as the Vice Chief of Naval Operations before retiring in 1995. Stan Arthur had checked into VA-164 as XO in July 1971, and 'fleeted up' to CO a year later.

Several 'Ghostrider' A-4Fs carried a Laser Spot Tracker (LST) in their nose cones, along with a Ferranti gun sight that could show the spot where the laser energy was directed. The problem with this arrangement was that the single-seat 'Foxtrot' pilot had to rely on a FAC, airborne or on the ground, to 'lase' the target. The Navy had developed a hand-held laser, which allowed the aircraft crew to pinpoint the target themselves, but the single-seater pilot could not fly the aircraft and handle the laser simultaneously. Another pair of hands was required, and the TA-4F was just the thing.

A VA-55 A-4F fires a Shrike anti-radiation missile during a training exercise (*via Lou Mortimer*)

VA-164 CO Cdr Stan Arthur checks the large wall map in the 'Ghostrider' ready room. His finger indicates that he is headed into North Vietnam. Starting out as a 'Stoof' pilot, flying S-2s, Arthur transitioned to A-4s and flew with VA-55, before joining VA-164 as XO in July 1971. He took command of VA-164 a year later

Arthur and his unit recruited other crewmen from the CVW-21 squadrons to man the rear seat. Originally, the most likely candidates were Naval Flight Officers (NFOs), usually found in F-4s and A-6s. However, as neither of these aircraft flew with CVW-21, the only NFOs came from the E-1B Tracer det, as well as the occasional pilot looking for a new combat experience. Some of the F-8 and RF-8 pilots tried it, but predictably they did not feel comfortable making an approach to the small flightdeck, trusting their safe recovery to another pilot up front. It would be the only time the two-seat Skyhawk saw combat from a carrier flightdeck.

Although blurred, this photograph is of particular interest because it is one of the very few taken of VA-164's TA-4Fs during the 1972 cruise aboard *Hancock*. BuNo 153491 had previously served with H&MS-11 (as seen on page 85) at Da Nang before being reassigned to the 'Ghostriders' (*Leon Bryant*)

On a particular mission against a bridge near Thanh Hoa (not the well known railway bridge), Arthur had his A-4Fs loaded with an incredible 5000 lbs of ordnance, including two 500-lb bombs on the outboard stations, two 1000-lb bombs on the inner stations and a huge 2000-lb Mk 84 on the centreline, replacing the normal 300-gallon fuel tank.

The strike plan called for a TA-4F to designate the target for the laser-guided bombs from another squadron, and the 'Ghostriders' would drop their ordnance visually. Adm Arthur recalled;

'It was a great bomb load with very little drag, so even with 2000 lbs (a gallon of gas weighs six pounds) of fuel missing, we could fly a fairly normal profile and get back with adequate fuel. Part of the reason we tried this load was our experience with the TA-4Fs. They used the double-bubble drop tank configuration, while the "straight" A-4 used a single tank on the centreline. We had started putting on a 1000-lb Mk 83 so the two-seater could deliver a punch if needed. It was a natural evolution to free up the centreline on a few birds for this strike.

'Of course, it was more complicated than it sounds. One drop tank and two TERs had to be deleted, then fitted back after the strike. There was then the risk that all the connections wouldn't be made right, and the next flight would have hung bombs or the drop tank wouldn't transfer. However, our ordnance gang was top notch, and we had no such problems on the next sorties.'

Pilots manned up to the sound of 'Ghostriders in the Sky', a popular song of the 1950s by Stan Jones relating a cowboy's encounter with spirits on horseback while riding the range. It was just the right sound to send them off as the driving tune piped over the flightdeck loudspeaker.

The strike was a success, and Stan Arthur got a direct hit, dropping his huge load in one salvo! Denny Sapp was flying as *Iron Hand*, and he orbited the striker group as it hit its target. No SAMs came up, and Sapp was free to film the attack with his 8 mm movie camera.

During the intense ground battle for An Loc shortly after the NVA invaded South Vietnam, Cdr Arthur and his flight supplied close air support for US troops. The shoulder-fired SA-7 SAM was causing concern, and the A-4s maintained a higher than normal altitude for releasing their ordnance. Although previous tactics during *Rolling*

Thunder did not allow for multiple runs, they were required during this new phase of the war because of the closeness of both sides on the ground. Accuracy was paramount to prevent killing friendly troops.

As Arthur's flight attacked the targets they had received from one FAC, another controller came on the frequency asking what type of ordnance the A-4s had, and whether they could see the large building in the city square? Cdr Arthur replied he saw the structure. The FAC said he was in the *basement*, and that the enemy was coming in on the ground level. He added his only hope for escape was if the Navy could hit the building with one bomb fused so that it would not go down into the basement. Fortunately, the flight had dual-fused bombs, which used both mechanical and electrical settings to detonate.

Arthur told the FAC there was no guarantee that the bombs could be depended on to detonate with the electrical fusing, and that they would default to the mechanical setting if the first method failed. All this meant that there was no sure bet that the bomb would not, in fact, go down to the basement where the FAC was hiding before exploding. The FAC nevertheless told Arthur to drop his ordnance, and to hurry up!

The XO acknowledged, rolled in and dropped his bomb, getting a direct hit – the bomb did go off instantaneously, which is what the FAC wanted. Arthur later mused;

'The question that is still unanswered is did he get out? A few years ago, I heard about an Army guy who got out of An Loc because he survived a bomb hit on a building he was hiding in. But I have no idea if that was true, and if so, was it that mission?'

THE MARINES RETURN

When US troop withdrawals started in 1969, Marine aviation also began sending squadrons home. Chu Lai was closed in July 1970, and the remaining units, including VMA-311 and H&MS-11 with its TA-4Fs, moved to Da Nang. The A-4s were kept busy supporting operations like *Lam Son 719* from the larger Air Force installation. VMA-311 flew hundreds of interdiction strikes, but by June 1971 all American units had left South Vietnam, and the North Vietnamese watched as the feared umbrella of US air power folded, leaving South Vietnam on its own.

Nine months later the North invaded the South, and along with other services, the Marines scrambled to reassemble their line-up of aviation units to push the enemy back over the 17th parallel. VMA-211 and VMA-311 flew into Bien Hoa air base, north-east of Saigon, on 17 May 1972. The A-4s had been divided between the main base at MCAS Iwakuni, in Japan, and NAS Cubi Point, in the Philippines, where they had been conducting work-ups before going to Vietnam. Two days later, there were 32 A-4s at Bien Hoa ready for combat once again.

From 19 May, the 'Tomcats' and 'Avengers' hit targets in South Vietnam and along the Cambodian border. On 11 June they supported units of the ARVN, and for nearly 13 hours Marine A-4s cycled in and out of Bien Hoa, which was also hit by enemy rockets.

Five H&MS-15 TA-4Fs had come from Japan during the build-up following the Easter Invasion, and they flew in the fast FAC role. Observers in the two-seat A-4s functioned as naval gunfire spotters and FACs, flying as many as four missions a day. On 26 May, the crew of an

VMA-311 was rushed back to South Vietnam following the Easter Invasion of March 1972. These 'Tomcat' A-4Es are protected by revetments at the USAF base at Da Nang. The aircraft in the right revetment is A-4E BuNo 152069, which subsequently served with VMA-311 at MCAS Iwakuni in 1973-74, before being handed over to VMA-211 at this location. Its final assignment was with Fleet Composite Squadron VC-5, based at NAS Cubi Point, in the Philippines

H&MS-15 TA-4F (BuNo 153508) found an NVA tank near Hue and strafed it with cannon fire. As they pulled up from their first run, their jet was hit by an SA-7. Capt W E Ramsbottom and observer CWO2 Bruce E Boltze flew the badly damaged Skyhawk back to Da Nang but had to eject over the water when ten miles from the field. Sadly, CWO2 Boltze was subsequently killed in October while flying in a USAF OV-10.

Meanwhile MAG-12's A-4 squadrons continued flying in support of the ground action, especially around the town of An Loc. Most of the MAG-12 Skyhawks' missions were within a radius of 50 miles from Bien Hoa, and often as close as three to five miles. The NVA was well aware of the presence of the Marine units, and it rocketed the base repeatedly. This meant that the Marines had to work closely with Air Force security personnel to ensure the safety of their installation.

On 26 September 1972, Capt James P Walsh of VMA-211 launched with his wingman toward An Loc. A FAC gave the two pilots their targets, and as they pulled out of their runs, Walsh's A-4E (BuNo 151099) was hit by ground fire. The A-4 began to shake and Walsh felt his controls go slack. His jet was throwing streams of flame from its tailpipe, and with red lights all around him in the cockpit, the young Marine aviator ejected. Walsh had ejected in the middle of an enemy encampment, and he was quickly surrounded. Deciding to fight capture, Walsh ran for his life, diving into a stream. However, as he surfaced, there was an enemy soldier waiting and Walsh was taken prisoner. He was the last Marine to be captured by the North Vietnamese, and was eventually released in 1973.

As 1972 wore on, the Marines sent several squadrons back to Japan, including the fast FAC det of H&MS-15 TA-4Fs. A large det, known as TF Delta, was sent to Nam Phong, in Thailand, to fly its F-4s and A-6s into North Vietnam. The two A-4 squadrons continued flying from Bien Hoa, VMA-311 attaining its 50,000th combat sortie of the war on 29 August. Operations continued through September and early October, even as the enemy maintained their sporadic rocketing of the facility.

MAG-12 finally pulled out of South Vietnam on 29 January 1973, by which time VMA-311 had racked up 54,625 combat sorties. Two days earlier, led by Col John Caldas, the 'Tomcats' delivered their last ordnance, appropriately painted in the squadron (also Marine Corps) colours of red and yellow. Caldas' bombs were rigged so that the 'special'

Lt Col John Caldas, CO of VMA-311, checks his load just before leading the very last combat sortie of the Vietnam War on 27 January 1973 from Bien Hoa. His A-4's bomb rack was configured so that the specially painted bomb shown here would be the last to drop minutes before the ceasefire took effect. The weapon's message read *THE LAST BOMB, 9,738.38 TONS DROPPED VMA-311, BIEN HOA, RVN 17 MAY 72-27 MAY 73*

A new SAM threat appeared in the final stages of the conflict in Vietnam in the form of the SA-3. It was a mobile, low-altitude missile that would enter service in increasing numbers throughout the communist bloc, including the Middle East (*via Istvan Toperczer*)

would be the last to go as they hit their final target – an ex-French rubber plantation north of Bien Hoa – a few minutes before the ceasefire came into effect at 1145 hrs local time. The A-4s then returned to Bien Hoa in a diamond formation.

FINAL MISSIONS FOR NAVY A-4s

As the war intensified over the summer, the men of CVW-21 found themselves heading into a longer than normal deployment. VA-55 had released a few pilots to rotate home, their period of service having reached its end. However, when Lt Tom Latendresse was shot down and captured on 27 May, the holes that were appearing in the squadron complement required that several other aviators be extended, among them Denny Sapp, who had been looking forward to detaching in June. Now, he and two other pilots were looking at a much longer war, with the accompanying danger of more missions.

As if to punctuate the problem, Lt Cdr Henry D Lesesne of VA-55 was shot down and captured on 11 July in A-4F BuNo 155046 while attacking a SAM site. Lesesne's jet had been hit by a missile, and he ejected into captivity.

VA-212's Lt W F Pear was flying an armed reconnaissance mission on 6 September in A-4F BuNo 155021 when he attacked several trucks and was hit by flak. With his aircraft on fire and the controls frozen, he had no choice but to eject – Pear was quickly rescued by helicopter. His was the last of 12 aircraft lost during *Hancock's* seventh combat cruise, and it was also the final Navy Skyhawk to go down during the war.

During the summer, *Hancock's* A-4s had followed the large strike packages – especially USAF B-52s – as they headed up into the hell that was the Hanoi-Haiphong flak-and-missile trap. It appeared that the communists would hold off firing, or even lighting up their radars, when they detected the *Iron Hand* A-4s detaching from the main group to head toward their assigned defence sites. The reputation of the A-4s and their Shrikes and Zunis had made it prudent for the enemy to shut down before they could be detected.

Capt Robert Hickerson was a Marine serving an exchange tour with VA-55. He had already completed a combat tour with VMA-223 and H&MS-11 in 1969. While assigned to VMA-324 (the first A-4M unit), Hickerson received orders to CVW-21 aboard *Hancock*.

He would be the first Marine assigned in a rebirth of an exchange programme that had been active prior to the Vietnam War.

Hickerson requalled in carrier landings and headed out to meet the carrier in the Philippines in June 1972. He immediately flew sorties into North Vietnam, often twice a day, before spending another shift as an LSO bringing his wingmates aboard. Near the end of the cruise, on 13 September, Hickerson went on an Alpha strike involving six divisions (24 aircraft) against the Thanh Hoa Bridge. As the section

leader of the last section, he was the 23rd jet to roll in on target. Flying A-4F BuNo 154194, he carried the 'big load' of 5000 lbs of ordnance;

'We used a high-altitude attack, and by the time it was my turn on the wagon-wheel roll-in, I could barely see the ground for smoke and dust from the bombs, flak and A-4s. When I got my nose pointed at the ground, I had at least four Skyhawks in my windshield coming from all directions, and lower in the attack. I finally got a good sight picture, pickled my bombs and started to pull up – it felt like the bombs had kept flying and the aeroplane had been ejected! I never got to do that again. The jet just leapt into the air when the Mk 84 separated.

'We went balls to the wall for the beach at more than 500 knots because we were clean. Listening to the checkouts on the strike freq, the photo-reconnaissance pilot in the RF-8 said we had dropped the bridge (this was

In 1969, Capt Bob Hickerson flew from Chu Lai with VMA-223 and from Da Nang with H&MS-11. In 1972, he flew an exchange tour with VA-55 aboard *Hancock*

The crewman scrambles out of the way as he signals all is ready for launch. This VA-55 A-4F (BuNo 154996) features a new ALR-45 homing and warning radar antenna atop its vertical tail – this equipment was a very late-war addition to the F-model. The aircraft is lightly armed with what appears to be a single Mk 82 on its centreline and one Mk 82 on each outer wing pylon. The two fuel tanks might indicate a long mission orbiting, waiting for a call either very late in the war or some time before 1975 when Seventh Fleet carriers kept a presence, but did not participate in further action. This photo also shows the late-build A-4F's kinked refuelling probe, which altered the usual straight probe to alleviate interference with the TIAS. An added benefit was the reduction of incidents involving ingestion of fuel into the intakes during inflight refuelling. Retired by VFC-12 in August 1993, this aircraft was supplied to the Argentine air force as a spares source for its A-4AR Fightinghawks in April 1997

The 'gang on the roof' takes some time out atop VA-164's A-4F BuNo 155018 *LADY JESSIE* during a break in the action in the 1971 war cruise – this jet also served as the CO's aircraft during the 1972 deployment. *Westpac* sailors enjoyed fostering a definite image during the war. These young enlisted men model the latest fashion in haircuts and beards. The restriction against such hirsute exhibitions was greatly relaxed during the Zumwalt period. Adm Elmo Zumwalt was the Chief of Naval Operations who permitted a much more liberal attitude toward regulations regarding dress and deportment, much to the chagrin of many more traditionally-minded members. Officers, too, let their beards and hair prosper, often treading the line between kempt and downright sloppy. Zumwalt's disruptive policies affected naval discipline, and most were ultimately rescinded by his more realistic successors. BuNo 155018 presently resides in the AMARC facility, having been one of seven A-4Fs retired by VF-126 in March 1994. The Pacific Fleet Adversary unit, which deactivated the following month, also sent three TA-4Js and a solitary TA-4F to Davis-Monthan AFB at the same time (*Denny Sapp*)

before the USAF with laser-guided bombs), so everyone was pretty happy as we headed back to the ship. Later, we learned that only some of the bridge's support structure had been destroyed. It lived on.'

Hickerson and the rest of the strike group flew back to *Hancock* on their remaining fuel, but the ship was not ready and deckcrew had to hastily clear the flightdeck for the big recovery. Hickerson trapped with just 400 lbs of fuel remaining.

'Amazingly, we managed to get everyone back aboard safely. *Hancock* and CVW-21 could really *operate* when the chips were down.'

The carrier A-4's war was essentially finished by this time. *Hancock* left the line in late September to begin the long trip back home. The veteran carrier would make two more cruises to South-east Asia beginning in May 1973 and ending in October 1975 with the same three VA units. But with the ceasefire of January 1973, and the return of those PoWs incarcerated in the known prisons, the Vietnam War came to a slow, grudging halt.

The 1973 cruise covered the minesweeping operations that cleared North Vietnamese waterways and harbours of the mines dropped by Navy and Marine aircraft the previous May. *Hancock* cut its stay in the South China Sea short, however, when it was sent to the Middle East as another Arab-Israeli war erupted in October. At one point there was some thought given to flying the carrier's A-4s and F-8s to Israel to augment the hard-pressed Israeli Defence Force/Air Force. *Hancock's* second, and final, post-war deployment to Vietnam covered the extraction of Americans and South Vietnamese as the communists finally conquered the South in April 1975.

LETTING THE NUMBERS SPEAK

More than 40 Navy and Marine Corps A-4 units (30 and 12, respectively) made at least one combat tour of Vietnam, with several chalking up seven and a few as many as eight. A large number of A-4 pilots survived injury and imprisonment over long years. Some did not make it home. Nine A-4 unit commanding officers were killed in action (including two who died as PoWs), with two other COs among the many Skyhawk pilots who served out those long periods of incarceration under harsh jailers. One A-4 pilot was also killed serving as air wing commander. A second CAG became a PoW, while another was shot down and recovered. One Marine aircraft group commander was shot down in a TA-4F and recovered.

A-4 pilots were among the most heavily decorated of the war, receiving many DFCs and Silver Stars. Six Navy Skyhawk pilots received the Navy Cross – the Navy's highest combat award. These awards were strictly for aerial action. At least one posthumous Navy Cross went to a Navy A-4 pilot for his conduct as a PoW. Lt James J Connell of VA-55 was shot down on 15 July 1966 and died while resisting barbarous treatment at the hands of the North Vietnamese. No Marine Corps A-4 pilot received

A gaggle of LSOs watches VA-212 A-4F BuNo 155012 return to *Hancock* on 21 May 1972. Although deck crewmen usually wear protective gear such as float coats (life preservers), LSOs have always eschewed such devices, and these young men are no exception. The only nod they may have made to such protection would have been some form of ear plugs. BuNo 155012 was destroyed in a flying accident on 24 January 1979 while serving with VC-7, based at NAS Miramar (*PH3 Jessie C Cralley*)

Crewmen send a message as *Hancock* steams for home at the end of its eventful 1972 war cruise

the Navy Cross. Three A-6 pilots were the only Marine jet aviators to receive the award. Surprisingly, their bombardier-navigators *sitting right beside them* during the actions received the 'lesser' Silver Star.

The only naval aviator flying a fixed-wing aircraft to receive the Medal of Honor (the highest US award for valour in combat) for an actual mission was an A-4 pilot, and that award was made posthumously. A Navy jet aviator did receive the Medal of Honor for his actions during his imprisonment – Cdr James B Stockdale had been flying an A-4 when he was shot down in September 1965.

More than 380 Skyhawks were lost in Vietnam – 12 percent of the total production run. Navy losses were 196 in combat and 77 operationally. The Marines lost 70 single-seat A-4s in combat and another 31 operationally. There were three fatalities in TA-4Fs, ten of which were lost in combat. Of the Navy fixed-wing aircraft lost in combat, 36 percent were A-4s. Marine Corps A-4 combat losses also amounted to 36 percent of all Marine Corps fixed-wing aircraft lost. Of all US fixed-wing aircraft lost in combat during the war, A-4s accounted for 11 percent.

By way of comparison, F-4s were 14 percent of the overall number of Navy combat losses, while Marine F-4s paralleled the Skyhawk with 36 percent, according to the Center for Naval Analyses. Navy A-4 crew losses were 98 killed in action and 48 PoW, whilst Marine Corps losses were 29 killed in action and one PoW.

In eight years of combat, Heinemann's little wonder had acquitted itself well. While overtaken by more advanced aircraft as the war progressed, the A-4 was, nonetheless, in action from beginning to end.

APPENDIX A

US NAVY A-4 SKYHAWK DEPLOYMENTS TO SOUTH-EAST ASIA FROM 1963 TO 1975

Squadron	Model	Ship	Air Wing	Dates
VA-12	A-4E	CVA-42	CVW-1	21 Jun 66 to 21 Feb 67
	A-4C	CVS-38	CVW-8	5 Mar 70 to 17 Dec 70
VA-15	A-4B	CVS-11	CVW-10	4 Apr 66 to 21 Nov 66
	A-4C	CVS-11	CVW-10	11 May 67 to 30 Dec 67
VA-22	A-4C	CVA-41	CVW-2	6 Mar 65 to 23 Nov 65
	A-4C	CVA-43	CVW-2	29 Jul 66 to 23 Feb 67
	A-4C	CVA-61	CVW-2	4 Nov 67 to 25 May 68
	A-4F	CVA-31	CVW-5	2 Apr 70 to 12 Nov 70
VA-23	A-4E	CVA-41	CVW-2	6 Mar 65 to 23 Nov 65
	A-4E	CVA-43	CVW-2	29 Jul 66 to 23 Feb 67
	A-4F	CVA-14	CVW-19	28 Dec 67 to 17 Aug 68
	A-4F	CVA-34	CVW-19	14 Apr 69 to 17 Nov 69
VA-34	A-4C	CVS-11	CVW-10	11 May 67 to 30 Dec 67
VA-36	A-4C	CVAN-65	CVW-9	26 Oct 65 to 21 Jun 66
	A-4C	CVS-11	CVW-10	4 Jun 68 to 8 Feb 69
VA-46	A-4E	CVA-59	CVW-17	6 Jun 67 to 15 Sep 67
VA-55	A-4E	CVA-14	CVW-5	14 Apr 64 to 15 Dec 64
	A-4E	CVA-61	CVW-14	10 Dec 65 to 25 Aug 66
	A-4C	CVA-64	CVW-14	29 Apr 67 to 4 Dec 67
	A-4F	CVA-19	CVW-21	18 Jul 68 to 3 Mar 69
	A-4F	CVA-19	CVW-21	2 Aug 69 to 15 Apr 70
	A-4F	CVA-19	CVW-21	22 Oct 70 to 3 Jun 71
	A-4F	CVA-19	CVW-21	7 Jan 72 to 3 Oct 72
VA-56	A-4E	CVA-14	CVW-5	14 Apr 64 to 15 Dec 64
	A-4E	CVA-14	CVW-5	28 Sep 65 to 13 May 66
	A-4C	CVAN-65	CVW-9	19 Nov 66 to 6 Jul 67
	A-4E	CVAN-65	CVW-9	3 Jan 68 to 18 Jul 68
VA-66	A-4C	CVS-11	CVW-10	4 Jun 68 to 8 Feb 69
VA-72	A-4E	CVA-62	CVW-7	10 May 65 to 13 Dec 65
	A-4E	CVA-42	CVW-1	21 Jun 66 to 21 Feb 67
VA-76	A-4C	CVAN-65	CVW-9	26 Oct 65 to 21 Jun 66
	A-4C	CVA-31	CVW-21	26 Jan 67 to 25 Aug 67
VA-86	A-4E	CVA-62	CVW-7	10 May 65 to 13 Dec 65
VA-93	A-4C	CVA-61	CVW-9	5 Aug 64 to 6 May 65
	A-4C	CVAN-65	CVW-9	26 Oct 65 to 21 Jun 66
	A-4E	CVA-19	CVW-5	5 Jan 67 to 22 Jul 67
	A-4F	CVA-31	CVW-5	27 Jan 68 to 10 Oct 68
VA-94	A-4C	CVA-61	CVW-9	5 Aug 64 to 6 May 65
VA-94 (cont.)	A-4C	CVAN-65	CVW-9	26 Oct 65 to 21 Jun 66
	A-4C	CVA-19	CVW-5	5 Jan 67 to 22 Jul 67
	A-4E	CVA-31	CVW-5	27 Jan 68 to 10 Oct 68
	A-4E	CVA-31	CVW-5	18 Mar 69 to 29 Oct 69
	A-4E	CVA-31	CVW-5	2 Apr 70 to 12 Nov 70
VA-106	A-4E	CVA-59	CVW-17	6 Jun 67 to 15 Sep 67
	A-4E	CVS-11	CVW-10	4 Jun 68 to 8 Feb 69
VA-112	A-4C	CVA-63	CVW-11	5 Nov 66 to 19 Jun 67
	A-4C	CVA-63	CVW-11	18 Nov 67 to 28 Jun 68
	A-4C	CVA-14	CVW-16	1 Feb 69 to 18 Sep 69
VA-113	A-4C	CVA-63	CVW-11	19 Oct 65 to 13 Jun 66
	A-4C	CVAN-65	CVW-9	19 Nov 66 to 6 Jul 67
	A-4F	CVAN-65	CVW-9	3 Jan 68 to 18 Jul 68
VA-113 Det Q	A-4B	CVS-20	CVSG-59	22 Mar 65 to 7 Oct 65
VA-144	A-4C	CVA-64	CVW-14	5 May 64 to 1 Feb 65
	A-4C	CVA-14	CVW-5	28 Sep 65 to 13 May 66
	A-4C	CVA-63	CVW-11	5 Nov 66 to 19 Jun 67
	A-4E	CVA-63	CVW-11	18 Nov 67 to 28 Jun 68
	A-4E	CVA-31	CVW-5	18 Mar 69 to 29 Oct 69
	A-4F	CVA-31	CVW-5	2 Apr 70 to12 Nov 70
VA-146	A-4C	CVA-64	CVW-14	5 May 64 to 1 Feb 65
	A-4C	CVA-61	CVW-14	10 Dec 65 to 25 Aug 66
	A-4C	CVA-64	CVW-14	29 Apr 67 to 4 Dec 67
VA-152	A-4E	CVS-38	CVW-8	5 Mar 70 to 17 Dec 70
VA-153	A-4C	CVA-43	CVW-15	7 Dec 64 to 1 Nov 65
	A-4C	CVA-64	CVW-15	12 May 66 to 3 Dec 66
	A-4E	CVA-43	CVW-15	26 Jul 67 to 6 Apr 68
	A-4F	CVA-43	CVW-15	7 Sep 68 to 18 Apr 69
VA-153 Det R	A-4B	CVS-33	CVSG-53	19 Jun 64 to 16 Dec 64
VA-155	A-4E	CVA-43	CVW-15	7 Dec 64 to 1 Nov 65
	A-4E	CVA-64	CVW-15	12 May 66 to 3 Dec 66
	A-4E	CVA-43	CVW-15	26 Jul 67 to 6 Apr 68
	A-4F	CVA-61	CVW-2	26 Oct 68 to 17 May 69
VA-163	A-4E	CVA-34	CVW-16	5 Apr 65 to 16 Dec 65
	A-4E	CVA-34	CVW-16	26 May 66 to 16 Nov 66
	A-4E	CVA-34	CVW-16	16 Jun 67 to 31 Jan 68
	A-4E	CVA-19	CVW-21	18 Jul 68 to 3 Mar 69
VA-164	A-4E	CVA-34	CVW-16	5 Apr 65 to 16 Dec 65
	A-4E	CVA-34	CVW-16	26 May 66 to 16 Nov 66
	A-4E	CVA-34	CVW-16	16 Jun 67 to 31 Jan 68
	A-4F	CVA-19	CVW-21	18 Jul 67 to 31 Jan 68
	A-4F	CVA-19	CVW-21	2 Aug 69 to 15 Apr 70

Squadron	Model	Ship	Air Wing	Dates
VA-164 (cont.)	A-4F	CVA-19	CVW-21	22 Oct 70 to 3 Jun 71
	A/TA-4F	CVA-19	CVW-21	7 Jan 72 to 3 Oct 72
VA-172	A-4C	CVA-42	CVW-1	21 Jun 66 to 21 Feb 67
	A-4C	CVS-38	CVW-8	5 Mar 70 to 17 Dec 70
VA-192	A-4C	CVA-31	CVW-19	28 Jan 64 to 21 Nov 64
	A-4C	CVA-31	CVW-19	21 Apr 65 to 13 Jan 66
	A-4E	CVA-14	CVW-19	15 Oct 66 to 29 May 67
	A-4F	CVA-14	CVW-19	28 Dec 67 to 17 Aug 68
	A-4F	CVA-34	CVW-19	14 Apr 69 to 17 Nov 69
VA-195	A-4C	CVA-31	CVW-19	28 Jan 64 to 21 Nov 64
	A-4C	CVA-31	CVW-19	21 Apr 65 to 13 Jan 66
	A-4C	CVA-14	CVW-19	15 Oct 66 to 29 May 67
	A-4C	CVA-14	CVW-19	28 Dec 67 to 17 Aug 68
	A-4E	CVA-34	CVW-19	14 Apr 69 to 17 Nov 69
VA-212	A-4E	CVA-19	CVW-21	21 Oct 64 to 29 May 65
	A-4E	CVA-19	CVW-21	10 Nov 65 to 1 Aug 66
	A-4E	CVA-31	CVW-21	26 Jan 67 to 25 Aug 67
	A-4F	CVA-31	CVW-5	27 Jan 68 to 10 Oct 68
	A-4F	CVA-19	CVW-21	2 Aug 69 to 15 Apr 70
	A-4F	CVA-19	CVW-21	22 Oct 70 to 3 Jun 71
	A-4F	CVA-19	CVW-21	7 Jan 72 to 3 Oct 72

Squadron	Model	Ship	Air Wing	Dates
VA-216	A-4C	CVA-19	CVW-21	21 Oct 64 to 29 May 65
	A-4C	CVA-19	CVW-21	10 Nov 65 to 1 Aug 66
	A-4C	CVA-43	CVW-15	7 Sep 68 to 18 Apr 69
VSF-3	A-4B	CVS-11	CVW-10	11 May 67 to 30 Dec 67

Carrier Key

CVS-11 - USS *Intrepid*
CVA-14 - USS *Ticonderoga*
CVA-19 - USS *Hancock*
CVS-20 - USS *Bennington*
CVA-31 - USS *Bon Homme Richard*
CVS-33 - USS *Kearsarge*
CVA-34 - USS *Oriskany*
CVS-38 - USS *Shangri-la*
CVA-41 - USS *Midway*
CVA-42 - USS *Franklin D Roosevelt*
CVA-43 - USS *Coral Sea*
CVA-59 - USS *Forrestal*
CVA-61 - USS *Ranger*
CVA-62 - USS *Independence*
CVA-63 - USS *Kitty Hawk*
CVA-64 - USS *Constellation*
CVAN-65 - USS *Enterprise*

APPENDIX B

US MARINE CORPS A-4 SKYHAWK DEPLOYMENTS TO SOUTH-EAST ASIA FROM 1963 TO 1975

Squadron	Model	Aircraft Group	Dates
VMA-121	A-4C	MAG-12	1 Dec 66 to 3 Jun 67
	A-4E		5 Sep 67 to 14 Feb 69
VMA-211	A-4E	MAG-12	11 Oct 65 to 14 Jul 66
			1 Oct 66 to 3 Sep 67
			1 Dec 67 to 25 Feb 70
			17 May 72 to 30 Jan 73
VMA-214	A-4C	MAG-12	21 Jun 65 to 16 Feb 66
			30 Apr 66 to 3 Apr 67
VMA-214 Det N	A-4B	CVS-12	9 Oct 63 to 15 Apr 64
VMA-223	A-4E	MAG-12	15 Dec 65 to 1 Dec 66
			2 Mar 67 to 3 Dec 67
			23 Apr 68 to 28 Jan 70
VMA-223 Det T	A-4C	CVS-10 (*Yorktown*)	23 Oct 64 to 16 May 65
VMA-224	A-4E	MAG-12	4 Oct 65 to 1 May 66
			14 Jul 66 to 1 Nov 66
VMA-225	A-4C	MAG-12	1 Jun 65 to 30 Sep 65
VMA-311	A-4E	MAG-12	1 Jun 65 to 16 Dec 65
			15 Feb 66 to 2 Mar 67
			4 Jun 67 to MAG-13

Squadron	Model	Aircraft Group	Dates
VMA-311 (cont.)		MAG-13	12 Feb 70 to MAG-11
		MAG-11	15 Apr 71 to 12 May 71
		MAG-12 (Bien Hoa)	17 May 72 to 30 Jan 73
H&MS-11	TA-4F	MAG-11	7 Jul 65 to 1 Jun 71
H&MS-12	TA-4F	MAG-12	25 May 65 to 25 Feb 70
H&MS-13	TA-4F	MAG-13	25 Sep 66 to 30 Sep 70
H&MS-15	TA-4F	MAG-15	16 Apr 72 to 20 Jun 72
H&MS-15 Det N	A-4C	CVS-12 (*Hornet*)	12 Aug 65 to 23 Mar 66
H&MS-16	TA-4F	MAG-15	6 May 65 to 20 Jun 71

Notes
H&MSs remained with their assigned MAGs and did not rotate home as did individual squadrons. H&MSs flew a variety of aircraft, including TA-4Fs when they became available in 1967 – H&MSs -11, -12 and -13 flew the majority of TA-4F sorties.

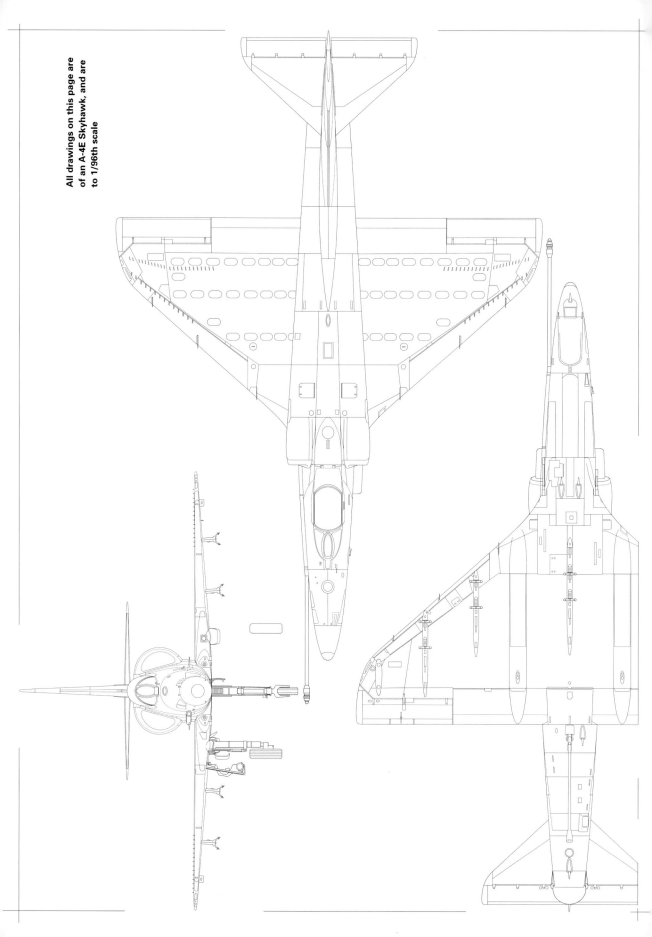

All drawings on this page are
of an A-4E Skyhawk, and are
to 1/96th scale

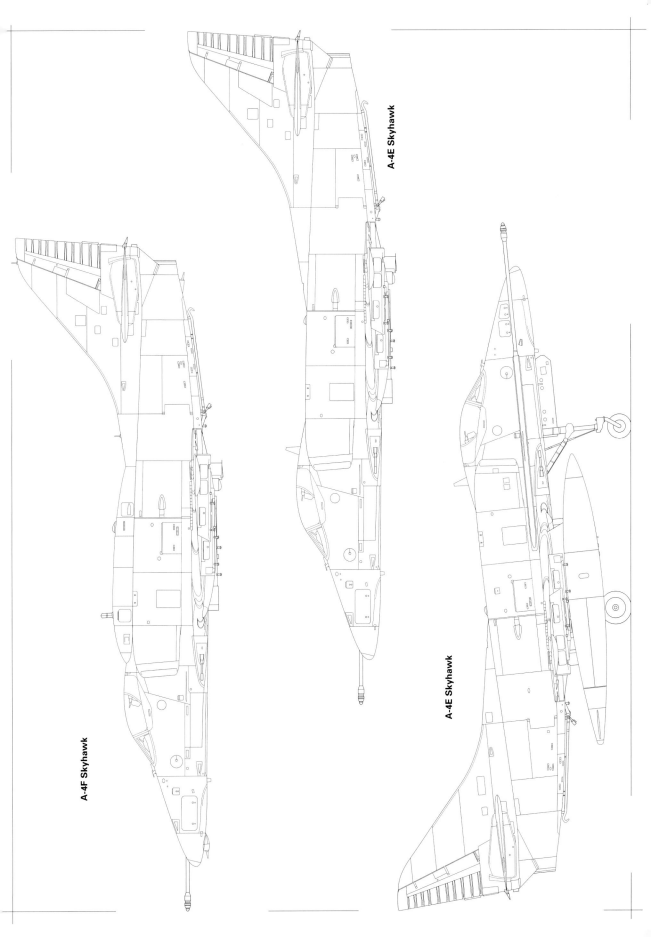

A-4E Skyhawk

A-4F Skyhawk

A-4E Skyhawk

COLOUR PLATES

1

A-4C BuNo 148609 of VA-12, USS *Shangri-la*, 1970
This aircraft is shown during an impromptu visit to NAS Atsugi in July 1970. CVW-8 aircraft went ashore while *Shangri-la* put in at Yokosuka to replace a damaged screw. Flying with VA-76 in May 1967, this jet, with Lt Cdr T R Swartz at the controls, downed a MiG-17. Possessing one of the most singular squadron insignia, VA-12 'Kiss of Death' made two war cruises, both in A-4s. Another unit nickname was 'The Flying Ubangis', and its unofficial, and by today's standards politically incorrect, insignia was a caricature of an African tribesman with a stretched neck and broad lips. See page 42 for this jet's operational history.

2

A-4F BuNo 154217 of VA-22, USS *Bon Homme Richard*, 1969
VA-22 'Fighting Redcocks' made six Vietnam combat deployments (four with the A-4 and two with the A-7) between March 1965 and November 1973. Two of these saw the unit flying A-4Fs from CVA-31 during the relatively quiet 1969-70 period – VA-22 did not lose a single jet on either cruise. Marked up in *Blue Angels* colours, BuNo 154217 is presently on display in the National Museum of Naval Aviation at NAS Pensacola, in Florida.

3

A-4E BuNo 151168 of VA-23, USS *Coral Sea*, 1966
VA-23 'Black Knights' completed four combat cruises embarked in four different carriers between March 1965 and November 1969. The first Navy squadron to lose an aircraft to a North Vietnamese SAM, when Lt(jg) D H Brown was shot down on the night of 11/12 August 1965, VA-23 had also become the first unit to use the anti-SAM Shrike missile (four of which are carried by this jet, illustrated in *Iron Hand* configuration) in combat four months earlier. BuNo 151168 was the 16th, and last, aircraft to be lost in action by CVW-2 during its 1966-67 cruise aboard CVA-43, the A-4 being downed by AAA on 15 January 1967. Although mortally wounded, pilot Lt(jg) Daniel Moran succeeded in reaching the Gulf of Tonkin prior to ejecting, but he was dead by the time a SAR destroyer pulled him out of the water.

4

A-4C BuNo 148528 of VA-36, USS *Intrepid*, 1968
VA-36 'Roadrunners' marked its jets with the silhouette of the Warner Bros cartoon character that inspired the unit's nickname. VA-36 completed two combat tours, with the first, in 1965-66, being made in conjunction with three other A-4 units as part of CVW-9's enlarged light strike component embarked in *Enterprise*. Subsequently switching to CVW-10, the 'Roadrunners' enjoyed the more 'snug' confines of *Intrepid* for their 1968-69 war cruise. See page 63 for BuNo 148528's history.

5

A-4F BuNo 155008 of VA-55, USS *Hancock*, April 1972
This jet is seen here with the external weapons load it carried on 12 April 1972 during the famous 'Bat 21' rescue mission. VAs -55, -164 and -212 each completed eight war cruises, thus making them the most battle-hardened light strike units in the Navy. BuNo 155008 was one of the A-4E/Fs pulled from frontline service in October 1973 and made available to Israel as attrition replacements.

6

A-4C BuNo 149497 of VA-56, USS *Enterprise*, 1967
This jet was assigned to the CO of VA-56, Cdr Ernest R Seymour, who had a 13-month command tour. It survived CVW-9's 1966-67 war cruise, returning to NAS Lemoore in July 1967 with 72 mission markings on its port intake. The 'Champs' were one of the first A-4 units to see action in Vietnam, participating in the Gulf of Tonkin Incidents of August 1964 under the command of Wesley L McDonald, who later rose to the rank of four-star admiral. BuNo 149497 was also sold to the Republic of Singapore Air Force in 1980.

7

A-4C BuNo 145122 of VA-66, USS *Intrepid*, 1969
Carrying a *Tonkin Gulf Yacht Club* patch on its tail, this aircraft is devoid of the pilot's name. However, the nickname *THE RAM* beneath the cockpit refers to unit CO, Cdr W E Ramsey, who led VA-66 from May 1968 to February 1969. Note also the bomb mission marking silhouette, with the number 91 above *THE RAM* panel. Nicknamed the 'Waldomen', VA-66 made just one Vietnam combat cruise. BuNo 145122 was one of 100 C-models upgraded to A-4L specification for the Navy Reserve in the 1970s, and it has been displayed atop a pole in the grounds of Savannah State College, Georgia, for a number of years.

8

A-4E BuNo 149993 of VA-72, USS *Independence*, 1965
An AIRLANT squadron, VA-72 was one of several east coast units that helped take up the added requirement as the Navy increased its participation in Vietnam. It made two combat deployments, one aboard 'Indy' and another in 'FDR'. See page 16 for the operational history of this aircraft.

9

A-4C BuNo 147843 of VA-76, USS *Bon Homme Richard*, May 1967
The 'Spirits' (of 1776) made two combat cruises to Vietnam – one aboard CVAN-65 (1965-66) and one in CVA-31 (1967). The pilot whose name appears on this jet assumed command – as a lieutenant commander – when Cdr R B Fuller was downed by a SAM on 14 July 1967 in A-4C BuNo 147709.

Lt Cdr R A Mauldin relinquished command in 1968, but returned the following year as a CO to lead the unit until it decommissioned in September 1969. Upgraded into an A-4L and issued to Reserve-manned VA-204, BuNo 147843 was lost in a mid-air collision with BuNo 149640 from the same unit on 6 March 1975.

10

A-4E BuNo 151105 of VA-93, USS *Hancock*, May 1967

With double wing tanks on inner stations 2 and 4, one Shrike on each outer wing station 1 and 5 and two Zuni pods on the centreline pylon, this jet is in a typical mid-war *Iron Hand* load-out. VA-93 lost five aircraft during this cruise, with four of the pilots becoming PoWs – the fifth was recovered. See page 45 for the operational history of this jet.

11

A-4C BuNo 149538 of VA-94, USS *Bon Homme Richard*, 1967

This jet features the unusual bomb load used for large Alpha strikes such as bridge-busting – an example is a strike against the Hai Duoung railway bridge between Haiphong and Hanoi – of three Mk 84 2000-lb bombs, one on each stores station (both wings and centreline). Such a configuration saw the jet launch with a greatly reduced fuel load, for no external tanks meant that the A-4 carried only 5400 lbs of fuel instead of the normal 9400 lbs. One or two inflight refuellings would therefore be required during the mission. BuNo 149538 was lost in an operational accident off the Florida coast on 31 July 1969 while serving with VA-36.

12

A-4E BuNo 152070 of VA-106, USS *Intrepid*, 1968

This aircraft is depicted in tanker configuration, with underwing fuel tanks and a centreline-mounted refuelling buddy store. Another AIRLANT unit to make a couple of war cruises, VA-106 lost more jets (four) in the *Forrestal* fire of 29 July 1967 than it did to the enemy (one, on 21 October 1968). BuNo 152070 is presently on display (as VA-46's BuNo 149996 which, ironically, was destroyed in the CVA-59 fire) in the Evergreen Aviation Museum complex in McMinnville, Oregon.

13

A-4C BuNo 147721 of VA-112, USS *Kitty Hawk*, 1968

VA-112 made three war cruises with the A-4C, and its 1967-68 deployment aboard CVA-63 was one of the last made by the A-4 on a 'big deck' carrier. See page 57 for the operational history of this jet.

14

A-4C BuNo 147847 of VA-113, USS *Enterprise*, 1966

This jet carried the name *CDR BOB BENNETT* beneath the cockpit, and as CO of VA-113 'Stingers', he was known as 'King Bee'! This aircraft was retired in the early 1970s and

eventually destroyed as a target on the Barry M Goldwater Range, in Arizona, in 1996.

15

A-4E BuNo 152029 of VA-144, USS *Bon Homme Richard*, 1969

Participating in the Gulf of Tonkin Incidents in 1964, VA-144 made a total of six war cruises in the A-4. BuNo 152029 was the only aircraft lost in combat by CVW-5 during its 1969 war cruise, Lt(jg) Leland Sage being killed when he flew the jet into the ground on 22 June during a night *Steel Tiger* attack on a target near Ban Soppeng, in Laos.

16

A-4C BuNo 147836 of VA-146, USS *Constellation*, July 1967

Cdr Robert Dunn received the Silver Star for his attack on a soccer stadium, which the enemy was using as a SAM site, in this jet on 19 July 1967. VA-146 was a busy unit, making seven combat deployments in A-4 and A-7s. BuNo 147836 was upgraded into an A-4L and finally retired by VC-2 to MASDC in September 1976. Although sold to Malaysia in 1983, the jet never left Arizona and was finally scrapped in Tucson in 2004.

17

A-4C BuNo 149574 of VA-153, USS *Coral Sea*, 1965

The only unit to see combat with 'Bravo', 'Charlie', 'Echo' and 'Foxtrot' models of the A-4, VA-153 made five Vietnam tours between June 1964 and April 1969. See page 15 for the history of this jet.

18

A-4E BuNo 151054 of VA-155, USS *Constellation*, 1966

Wearing three-tone camouflage in olive and blue/green vertical swathes, this aircraft is configured as a tanker, with two underwing drop tanks. Another veteran A-4 unit, VA-155 was one of those tapped for the short-lived camouflage experiment. This jet had been repainted in Navy grey and white by the end of CVA-64's 1966 cruise in December, when it was passed on to VMA-211. BuNo 151054 was written off when it suffered engine failure on take-off from Chu Lai on 24 July 1967. Its unnamed pilot survived the accident.

19

A-4E BuNo 151191 of VA-163, USS *Oriskany*, August 1967

Cdr Bryan Compton flew this all-Walleye loaded A-4E on the 21 August 1967 mission that earned him his Navy Cross. The 'Saints' were one of the hardest-working light attack squadrons of the conflict, making four combat cruises (all with the A-4E) during periods of the most intense action of the war – April 1965 to March 1969. BuNo 151191 was transferred to VMA-211 upon VA-163's disestablishment on 1 July 1971, and the A-4 was written off when it suffered engine failure on take-off from Bien Hoa on 9 November 1972. Its unnamed pilot survived the accident.

20
A-4F BuNo 155022 of VA-164, USS *Hancock*, 1969
The tradition of naming the 'Ghostrider' CO's jet *LADY JESSIE* derived from the close bond between VA-164's Lt Cdr Richard C Perry and Mrs Jessie Beck of Reno, Nevada. Mrs Beck owned a casino favoured by naval aviators (the Fallon target complex, 60 miles east of Reno, hosted air wings about to deploy). She befriended Dick Perry, then attending the University of Nevada, Reno, when he worked as a part-time dealer. When Perry got his naval aviator wings, none were more proud then the Becks, who sent care packages to the unit filled with food. Perry named his A-4 for Mrs Beck, and after he was killed in action in August 1967, VA-164 continued the tradition. Mrs Beck died in 1987 – the same year Perry's remains were returned by the Vietnamese. BuNo 155022 was transferred to VA-164 by VA-153 in Japan in March 1969 upon the completion of the latter unit's last A-4 cruise, embarked in CVA-43. The jet was retired to AMARC by adversary unit VFC-12 in August 1993, where it remains in storage today.

21
TA-4F BuNo 153491 of VA-164, USS *Hancock*, 1972
The unit's handful of TA-4s always launched with two tanks and, occasionally, one Mk 83 1000-lb bomb on the centreline. This jet had originally served in-country with H&MS-11 (see Profile 27).

22
A-4C BuNo 149621 of VA-172, USS *Shangri-la*, 1970
East coast squadron VA-172 made just two combat cruises – aboard 'FDR' and *Shangri-la* – prior to disestablishing in 1971. Wearing CAG colours on its rudder, this particular jet was sent to MASDC in November 1972 and eventually scrapped.

23
A-4E BuNo 151073 of VA-192, USS *Ticonderoga*, April 1967
This aircraft was lost during an *Iron Hand* mission on 26 April 1967 while being flown by Lt Cdr Michael J Estocin. The pilot's exploits on this sortie, and a similar mission a week before, combined to bring Estocin a posthumous Medal of Honor – the only one given for aerial action to a fixed-wing Naval Aviator during Vietnam. Note that this aircraft is one of the 'humped' 'Echos' with the avionics dorsal pack normally associated with the later 'Foxtrot'. It had previously served with VA-155 during a 1966 Vietnam deployment aboard CVA-64. The avionics hump was retrofitted when it joined VA-192 for its final cruise.

24
A-4E BuNo 151113 of VA-212, USS *Bon Homme Richard*, March 1967
As often happened during the war, one unit in a wing specialised in a specific area. VA-212 were the Walleye specialists for CVW-21. The squadron made seven combat deployments, all with A-4s,

eventually disestablishing in 1975. A small but dramatic indication of the intensity of the action at this point is the empty name panel beneath the cockpit. Although the author and artist have expended much effort determining the names below specific cockpits, the panel was often empty, as in this case. Photos of this jet distinctly show the yellow panel without a name. The 'luxury' of maintaining names and individual markings was often low on the list of squadron priorities. As long as jets flew their scheduled sorties and brought their pilots back, internal maintenance was infinitely more important than the cosmetic kind. Replacement A-4s flown in from Japan and the Philippines were quickly scheduled for missions, and painting names and insignia had to be accomplished when time permitted. This A-4 was downed by flak near Kep on 31 May 1967, its pilot, Lt Cdr A R Chauncey, becoming a PoW.

25
A-4C BuNo 148505 of VA-216, USS *Coral Sea*, 1968
The 'Black Diamonds' made three combat deployments (all with A-4Cs), flying some of the first sorties after the Gulf of Tonkin Incidents. Having survived Vietnam, this BuNo 148505 was upgraded into an A-4L and issued to the Navy Reserve (unit unknown). It was written off in a flying accident in New Mexico on 2 March 1976.

26
A-4B BuNo 142687 of VSF-3, USS *Intrepid*, 1967
The VSF concept was short-lived, but the one squadron that deployed to Vietnam was a colourful group, and saw action in what could only be considered at best an obsolescent aircraft. Note in this port side view that the wing cannon has been deleted to make room for extra ECM gear. BuNo 142687 served briefly with the Navy Reserve in a training capacity as a TA-4B in the late 1960s, after which it was sent to MASDC in May 1970.

27
TA-4F BuNo 153491 of H&MS-11, Da Nang, 1969
This jet carries the name of Col J B Heffernan (MAG-11 CO between August and December 1969) beneath its cockpit. Also note the Playboy bunny logo over its tailcode, as well as the hexagonal styled modex '00' on nose and tail. This reflected the calling of CAG/MAG CO aircraft 'double nuts'. See page 85 for the operational history of this jet.

28
A-4E BuNo 151050 of VMA-121, Chu Lai, 1966
This aircraft is armed with Mk 82 Snakeyes and World War 2-era Mk 117 750-lb bombs. The latter weapon was a holdover from World War 2 and the Korean War, and was used by the Air Force, Marines and Navy. Its rotund shape made the bomb stand out against the more streamlined, modern Mk 80 series that saw so much use in Vietnam. BuNo 151050 ended its days flying as fleet adversary with VF-45, before being retired to AMARC in March 1994 and scrapped in 2004.

29

A-4E BuNo 151147 of VMA-211, Chu Lai, 1968
VMA-211 completed four combat tours between October 1965 and January 1973, making it one of the most combat experienced light strike units in the Marine Corps. This jet was one of a number of A-4E/Fs supplied to Israel in 1973-74.

30

A-4C BuNo 147816 of VMA-223 Det T, USS
Yorktown, **1965**
While VMA-223 flew A-4Es from Chu Lai, in South Vietnam, 'Bulldog' Det T flew four C-models from the ageing *Yorktown*, now designated as an ASW carrier, as its air defence element. The six det pilots accumulated a record 1200 traps during the cruise using only four aircraft. Details of BuNo 147816's final fate can be found on page 44.

31

A-4E BuNo 150062 of VMA-224, Chu Lai, September 1966
VMA-224 was the Marine Corps' first A-4 unit, and it completed two tours in Vietnam between October 1965 and November 1966. Transferred to VMA-311 in the late 1960s, BuNo 150062 was shot down by AAA while attacking a target near Kontum, in the Central Highlands region of Vietnam, on 7 June 1970. Its pilot, Capt Fred Palka, ejected and was rescued by an Army helicopter.

32

A-4C BuNo 147767 of VMA-225, Chu Lai, 1965
Aside from its centreline fuel tank and Mk 83 1000-lb bombs on its underwing pylons, this jet also carried JATO bottles on its rear fuselage. VMA-225 was one of the first A-4 units to arrive at Chu Lai, and its aircraft often had to use JATO to help them get airborne from the base's unfinished strip. See page 79 for the operational history of this jet.

Back Cover

A-4E BuNo 151124 of VMA-311, Chu Lai, 1967
This jet is heavily loaded with Snakeyes and napalm canisters. VMA-311 was one of the most active Marine A-4 units in Vietnam, and eventually flew the last combat sorties of the war. BuNo 151124 was one of six A-4Es blown up at Chu Lai by VC sappers on the night of 21 March 1969.

COLOUR SECTION

1

A-4C BuNo 147816 from VMA-223's Det T recovers aboard CVS-10 in 1965. It carries two AIM-9s for CAP duties – Det T's primary mission (*D Siegfried*)

2

A mechanic works on a VA-93 A-4C. Although a simple jet, like all shipboard aircraft on cruise, the Skyhawk required constant attention during demanding combat operations in the high humidity and salty air of the South China Sea

3

A line of VA-72 A-4Es 'watches' a deckcrewman tend to the No 2 catapult on CVA-62 during the 1965 cruise – the only combat cruise 'Indy' made

4

VA-113's A-4C BuNo 148458 returns to CVA-63 in April 1966 after a strike on VC positions in South Vietnam. Note that to maintain the camouflage effect as viewed from above, the noses of the fuel tanks are also green. The jet's centreline MERs were routinely seen during this period of the war

5

Cdr Wynn Foster in 'AH 301' (top) leads 'AH-303' north in July 1966 – the month he was badly wounded. The jets carry a full load of Mk 82s

6

Probably carrying only the one Walleye shown in this view, VA-212's A-4E BuNo 151113 waits for a tow to the catapult in March 1967. While two Walleyes were occasionally carried, photos show this aircraft, at least on this sortie, with one missile under the starboard wing, and a Mk 82 500-lb bomb under the port wing for balance. This jet was shot down a month later and its pilot imprisoned

7

Seen for the first time in an unofficial publication, this photograph is one of several taken by a squadronmate of Al Crebo's battered VA-212 A-4E as he struggles to get back to his carrier on 25 April 1967. A SAM hit has blown away his rudder and several access panels. With his landing gear still up, Crebo is heading for the coast trailing fuel

8

VA-144 A-4E BuNo 152029 heads for targets in June 1969 (*Lt Cdr Stan Thompson*)

9

VA-55's A-4F NP 510 orbits off the DMZ, waiting a call to go in to support the rescue of a USAF EB-66 crewman 'Bat 21' on 12 April 1972 (*Denny Sapp*)

10

VA-55 A-4F NP 515 drops its Mk 82 Snakeyes

11

A-4E BuNo 151088 of VMA-211 gets the launch signal on the Chu Lai SATS catapult. This jet was lost to AAA on 11 August 1967, pilot 1Lt Ken Berube being killed when it crashed near Hiep Duc

12

VMA-211 A-4E BuNo 151096 waits for the start of flight operations soon after dawn at Chu Lai in 1969 (*L Wiseman*)

13

Bombed up and ready, A-4E BuNo 149658 of VMA-211 waits in its revetment at Chu Lai (*R Rivers*)

INDEX

References to illustrations are shown in **bold**. Plates are shown with page and caption locators in brackets.